RECEIVED

D0498342

NO LONGER PROPERTY OF
SEATTLE PUBLIC LIBRARY

"Dr. Boss clearly wrote this book in a manner that will appeal to parents, academics, clinicians, and students. Her examples of global losses are sobering and timely. She openly discloses that she penned this book in the wake of a personal loss—the death of her dear husband. When describing his passing, Dr. Boss noted: 'I am knocked down. And I will get up again.' I clung to the words 'will get up again'—realizing it was her way of sharing that she is still in the process of making her way up. That context makes this book even more poignant than all of her others."

—**Chalandra M. Bryant, Ph.D.**, Professor

"*The Myth of Closure* is a must-read for anyone and everyone who has experienced a loss or anticipates experiencing one. The book is not a therapy book, and yet it does meet the author's expectation of being quite therapeutic. Of all the books and articles that Dr. Boss has written throughout her illustrious career devoted to her pioneer work on ambiguous loss, this publication may be her finest. The book is timely and exactly what so many of us desperately need as we try to comprehend, adjust to, and gradually bounce back from the devastating losses that so many of us have experienced as we live amid a global pandemic. Boss's thesis regarding the myth of closure relative to loss was not only therapeutic but emotionally liberating, healing, and permission giving. I am convinced that this book will provide a much-needed compass to those who feel directionless following the loss of loved ones during the pandemic, and for whom 'proper closure' was not humanly possible due to COVID-related constraints. Boss reassures us that there is no such thing as closure to loss and grief, especially regarding those that are ambiguous. She provides an insightfully fresh and innovative approach to coming to terms with loss, grief, and the myth of closure. One of the most refreshing and welcomed features of this masterfully written book centers around Boss's expansion of her previous groundbreaking work on ambiguous loss to include a critical examination of global issues such as climate change and racism. If there were ever a time where a book with such a sharp focus was needed, one that speaks honestly, authoritatively, and eloquently to where we are as a nation and a world, it is now. We are indeed living in a time of significant and unparalleled loss where it is reassuring and comforting to know that there is an insightful guide available to help us, as Boss notes, 'move forward after traumatic loss and change.' This book is written for you and me, students and faculty, clinicians and non-clinicians, and anyone who needs a new and innovative way to conceptualize loss and grief. It is an easy read and replete with fresh ideas and wisdom regarding how to establish the resiliency to live with loss. There is no better time than now to add *The Myth of Closure: Ambiguous Loss in a Time of Pandemic and Change* to your reading list."

—**Kenneth V. Hardy, Ph.D.**, Clinical and Organizational Consultant, The Eikenberg Institute for Relationships, New York, New York

"As we deal with the ambiguous losses we are experiencing in the pandemic, Boss reminds us that while grief is a lifelong journey, we still have opportunities both to build resilience and grow from loss—even those losses that are unclear. The key to coping with ambiguous loss is 'both/and' thinking—accepting the loss as well as recognizing that things are still here. What we have lost is gone, but we continue to retain an emotional and spiritual bond with it. As Boss notes, this is a most important insight as we live through this pandemic. Her work is a is a *tour de force* that unites her earlier writings on loss, trauma, and resilience and it is a hopeful message to all of us who struggle to make sense of today's world."

—**Kenneth J. Doka, Ph.D.**, Senior Consultant, The Hospice Foundation of America, and Professor Emeritus, The College of New Rochelle

"From her own professional and personal experience, Boss offers us lessons in dealing with ambiguous loss. She writes beautifully and with great emotion as she tackles one of our most difficult challenges—how to grow through pain and suffering. Boss is a cultural therapist whose work helps us understand ourselves and each other."

—**Mary Pipher**, psychologist and author of *Women Rowing North* and *Reviving Ophelia*

THE MYTH OF CLOSURE

A Norton Professional Book

THE MYTH OF CLOSURE

AMBIGUOUS LOSS *in a Time of* PANDEMIC *and* CHANGE

PAULINE BOSS, PHD

AUTHOR OF THE CLASSIC
*AMBIGUOUS LOSS: LEARNING TO
LIVE WITH UNRESOLVED GRIEF*

W. W. NORTON & COMPANY
Independent Publishers Since 1923

Important Note: THE MYTH OF CLOSURE is intended to provide general information on the subject of health and well-being; it is not a substitute for medical or psychological treatment and may not be relied upon for purposes of diagnosing or treating any condition or illness. Please seek out the care of a professional healthcare provider if you are experiencing symptoms of any potentially serious condition. As of press time, the URLs displayed in this book link or refer to existing sites. The publisher and author are not responsible for any content that appears on third-party websites.

Copyright © 2022 by Pauline Boss

All rights reserved
Printed in the United States of America
First Edition

Frontis art by mreco99 / Depositphotos

For information about permission to reproduce selections from this book, write to Permissions, W. W. Norton & Company, Inc., 500 Fifth Avenue, New York, NY 10110

For information about special discounts for bulk purchases, please contact W. W. Norton Special Sales at specialsales@wwnorton.com or 800-233-4830

Manufacturing by Lakeside Book Company
Production manager: Gwen Cullen

Library of Congress Cataloging-in-Publication Data

Names: Boss, Pauline, author.
Title: The myth of closure : ambiguous loss in a time of pandemic / Pauline Boss, Ph.D.
Description: First edition. | New York, NY : W.W. Norton & Company, [2022] | Includes bibliographical references.
Identifiers: LCCN 2021014693 | ISBN 9781324016816 (hardcover) | ISBN 9781324016823 (epub)
Subjects: LCSH: Loss (Psychology) | Despair. | Uncertainty. | Resilience (Personality trait) | COVID-19 (Disease)—Psychological aspects.
Classification: LCC BF575.D35 B676 2022 | DDC 155.9/3—dc23
LC record available at https://lccn.loc.gov/2021014693

W. W. Norton & Company, Inc., 500 Fifth Avenue, New York, N.Y. 10110
www.wwnorton.com

W. W. Norton & Company Ltd., 15 Carlisle Street, London W1D 3BS

1 2 3 4 5 6 7 8 9 0

For my darling husband,
Dudley Riggs (1932–2020),
beloved by so many, and by me.

And for the millions of others who
experienced loss during this time of pandemic.
May you find solace in this book.

Like enduring a lesson that one is resisting,
I learned with each loss that "getting over it" was not
possible. I now walk with the tension of imperfect
solutions and balance them with the joys and passions
in my daily life. I intentionally hold the opposing
ideas of absence and presence, because I have learned
that most human relationships are indeed both.

Adapted from *Loss, Trauma, and Resilience: Therapeutic Work with Ambiguous Loss* (W. W. Norton, 2006), p. 210, by Pauline Boss.

Contents

Acknowledgments

This book was born not only from my 40 years of clinical and academic work, but also from my personal experiences of loss. Both were shaped by the times I lived in, from the Great Depression of the 1930s to the present. Now in my late 80s, I meld the personal with the professional and hope that both may be useful to you at this time of massive loss from the pandemic.

The ideas for *The Myth of Closure* came to me while I was working with families, clinically and around the world, all suffering with some kind of ambiguous loss. I saw that closure after loss isn't possible nor wanted in many cultures. I also learned that there is often some ambiguity in death as well. More recently, I'm told that the ambiguous loss lens is useful for understanding the urgency of more global losses—racism, for example, and climate change.

There are many who made this book possible. To my editor, Deborah Malmud, vice president at W. W. Norton & Company, I am deeply grateful to you for accepting my book proposal and for being my editor. I thank you for your expert direction and guidance in shaping this book—made especially challenging by constantly shifting circumstances during a time of pandemic and political upheaval.

In this book, any personal stories other than my own are included with the permission of the real people they are about. Each has written their own books, so theirs are already public stories. I thank Sarah Johnson, Donna Carnes, and David Francis for allowing me to hear and read their painful stories of ambiguous loss and trauma.

I especially thank Donna Carnes for coauthoring an article with me in 2012 for the clinical journal *Family Process* titled "The Myth of Closure." It is the forerunner of this book.

I thank Marly Rusoff and Philip Turner for feedback on early versions of my proposal. Although the book has changed its course, I value your early support.

I thank The Loft in Minneapolis, a center for writers, for offering me a quiet place to think and write the early drafts of this book.

For reading earlier versions of the manuscript and providing valuable feedback, I am grateful to clinical and academic colleagues and friends William Allen, Chalandra Bryant, Susan Conlin, Carla Dahl, Noriko Gamblin, Gail Hartman, Lori Kaplan, Tai Mendenhall, Erin Sheffels, Carol and Paul Riggs, Margaret Shryer, and Paul and Lisa Von Drasek.

For taking my photograph during the pandemic, and thus needing to do this outdoors in winter weather, I thank Stephan Kistler, retired scientist, professional photographer, and friend.

To the thousands of individuals and families I have worked with since the 1970s, I thank you for teaching me about ambiguous loss and the myth of closure. I am deeply grateful. You changed my life and my way of thinking, much of which is reflected in this book.

To the new generations of researchers, mental health practitioners, and humanitarian practitioners around the world who are now continuing to test the theory of ambiguous loss and its applications cross-culturally and applying it in new ways to help people understand global losses, I give you my deepest thanks and cheer you on. After all, theories are social constructions and need testing over time to determine their validity and usefulness. Thank you for continuing this necessary scientific process.

To my assistant, Carol Mulligan, with whom I have worked for 17 years, I give my profound thanks. Her assistance in formatting, fact checking, organizing references and notes, and, frankly, typing better than I do makes my writing possible. She is superbly skilled and a blessing to work with. I thank you, Carol, for assisting me with all my books, and with this book in particular, made more difficult by the pandemic's impact.

For their constant love and support, I thank my son, Dave Boss, and my daughter, Ann Boss Sheffels, MD. Since they were children, I have been writing books and papers, ironically being psychologically absent for them at times. I could not have done the writing back then, nor now, without their loving care and encouragement. Now, their children also cheer me on and help with editing and technical questions. For making me a proud grandmother and for their support and help, I thank Erin Sheffels, PhD; Sara Sheffels; Hayley Boss; and Christopher Sheffels.

My husband was here when I began this book but gone before I finished. He will not see my dedication, but he knew it was coming. We always discussed our writings with one another, and I miss that terribly. But there is some new hope now for all of us who survived, and I am content.

Preface

Some time ago, before the pandemic, I heard a guest panel on TV discussing news that the body of a missing crime victim had at last been found. One of the participants said it was good that the family would now have "closure." The host, Anderson Cooper, immediately objected and said that closure was just "a made-up media word." For me, his criticism was a refreshing departure from the media norm. Likely Cooper had learned that there is no such thing as closure from the pain of personal experiences—the death of his father when he was 10, the suicide of his brother, and most recently, the death of his mother.

Still today, many media personalities and journalists use the term "closure" as the essential feel-good ending to a painful story—satisfying perhaps for their viewers or readers, but not for people who know from experience that closure is a myth. While simplistic declarations of closure are comforting for bystanders, they are hurtful for the bereaved. If we have loved, we will want to remember. We can do this even while moving forward in a new way.

This idealization of closure was and still is playing a part in the denial of this pandemic, with too many saying, "It's a hoax. There's no danger. I don't have to wear a mask. I don't need to stay away from large crowds." While pandemic deniers are not using the term "closure," their actions reflect their beliefs in it. Case closed, no danger, absolute thinking.

My point is this: Continuing to use the term "closure" perpetuates the myth that losses and grief have a prescribed time for ending—or never starting—and that it's emotionally healthier to close the door on suffering than to face it and learn to live with it.

Research shows that we do better to live with grief than to deny it or close the door on it. Our task now, after a time of so much suffering, is to acknowledge our losses, name them, find meaning in them, and let go of the quest for closure. Instead of searching for closure, we search for meaning and new hope. We begin this search by becoming aware of family losses even from years ago. As Anderson Cooper said, this time in a *60 Minutes* interview with Joaquin Phoenix, discussing the actor's loss of his brother, River Phoenix, "There's no timeline for grief." Thank you, Anderson Cooper, for educating the public.

I've watched late-night talk shows since Jack Paar and Dick Cavett were hosts and so was listening when Stephen Colbert was talking with then Vice President Joe Biden about loss. Both men had experienced multiple traumatic losses in their youth, and yet, both seem to have found ways to live well without closure. They can speak easily, though tenderly, about those losses today. In another interview, this time with Anderson Cooper, Colbert, ever the fan of Tolkien, mused, "It's a gift to exist, and with existence comes suffering. There's no escaping that. . . . . I don't want it to have happened. I want it to *not* have happened, but if you are grateful for your life—which I think is a positive thing to do, not everybody is, and I'm not always, but it's the most positive thing to do—then you have to be grateful for all of it. You can't pick and choose what you're grateful for." Clarifying that the quote originated with *The Lord of the Rings* author J. R. R. Tolkien, the two men continued their candid and heartfelt talk about both of their tragic losses years ago. There is no possibility of closure for those we loved and lost, but we can learn to live with them and move forward while remembering.

This book is not a therapy book, but I hope it is therapeutic for anyone who wants to learn about the nuances of loss, its lack of closure, and what helps us live with its ambiguity and not knowing. When ambiguous losses can't be prevented, it is resilience, not closure, that provides us with new hope and the strength to live life in a new way. In this time of great loss from the pandemic, there will be no closure. The stories of loss will be passed down across generations. Hopefully, they will be stories of both loss and resilience.

That closure is a myth is an idea I may have learned when I was a child growing up in an immigrant family. But I learned that lesson more clearly at age 19, with my first major loss. My little brother, for whom I was like a junior mother, died of bulbar polio during the epidemic of the

1950s. I think of him still. He died, and we had a death certificate and a funeral, but I still had so many unanswered questions. I still do. But the idea of naming this phenomenon "ambiguous loss" didn't come to me until I was a doctoral student at the University of Wisconsin–Madison. I was a homemaker (as it was called then) going back to school, studying human development, specifically father absence in intact families—and came up with the term "psychological father absence in intact families." My professor told me I was on the right track but needed to find a more general term, as my idea was about more than fathers. I went home and thought about it for some time, and eventually came up with the term "ambiguous loss." The rest is history.

Later in my life, I wondered why I was thinking about psychological father absence and realized I had lived with it as a child. My father emigrated from Switzerland in 1929 and was cut off from his beloved mother and siblings due to the Great Depression and then World War II. Not even phone calls were allowed until the war was over. As far back as I can remember, I saw him sad when letters came, especially with black borders on them, meaning that someone in his family had died. I could feel he had other people he loved—a family across the ocean—but I did not know them. It was his immigrant homesickness—and also that of my Swiss maternal grandmother—that first taught me about ambiguous loss. It was all around me in my childhood.

What surprised me when I named that phenomenon was how universal it was and how helpful people said it was to understand that they could live with ambiguity, that they did not need closure. I was also surprised at how many different kinds of ambiguous loss there are—from catastrophic (like the 2020 pandemic) to more common and everyday separations from breakups, divorces, adoptions, or leaving home due to immigration and migration.

Ambiguous loss is neither a disorder nor a syndrome, but simply a framework to help us understand the complexity and nuances of loss and how to live with it. My focus is on building resilience to live with and thrive despite a loss that can't be clarified. Here, resilience means increasing your tolerance for ambiguity.

As a result of the great uncertainty that surrounded the COVID-19 pandemic, the ambiguous losses skyrocketed and left some lasting effects for us to deal with for years to come, as individuals and as a collective. While I write from an American perspective, the ideas in this book about closure, ambiguous loss, grief, and social injustice can be applied across cultures and adapted globally. Wherever they are, I write for the millions who are still unmoored by their pandemic losses and want to make sense of them.

With so many sickened and dead worldwide, we are just now emerging from this great shadow of death. Life will go on, but it will be different. It already is. We won't go back to the way we were because change is both needed and taking place. What we need to do now is to reflect on all that just happened, what losses we had, how we are dealing with them, and how we, personally, as a nation, and as a global community can move forward in a new way. What helps? Letting go of the idea of closure and instead, finding meaning in our losses; thinking both/and about the positive and negative; increasing our tolerance for ambiguity; and finally, risking change by doing something different.

■ ■ ■

The book is organized to help you move forward after traumatic loss and change. Because we need to understand ambiguous loss before being able to understand why closure is a myth, I begin with a review and update about ambiguous loss in Chapter 1. It will help you understand what ambiguous loss is, and how it helps you to see that closure is a myth, unhelpful and unattainable.

Chapter 2 presents my ideas about closure as a myth and my frustration with the continuing use not only of that term, but also of the idea that if you work hard enough, you can get over your grief. No, you can't. But you can learn to both live with loss and have a good life.

Chapter 3 discusses that along with the pandemic, another global problem is now more visible: racism. Ambiguous loss and the myth of closure both have relevance for racism and cross-generational trauma where there is no closure. We can no longer deny the many losses due to racism today, nor the cross-generational trauma that has no closure.

Chapter 4 is about resilience, perhaps the best hope for us in painful situations that have no immediate solution.

Chapter 5 encourages coping with loss by accepting the paradox of absence and presence.

Chapter 6 suggests a new way of thinking to lower your distress after loss.

Chapter 7 describes six guidelines for building resilience to live with loss, both ambiguous and clear.

Chapter 8 describes what normal grief is and points out that we can also learn about grief from the personal writings of our teachers.

Chapter 9 turns toward the future and discusses change, the stress of it, and its necessity for survival after the trauma and loss we have experienced during the pandemic and now.

May you find this book helpful in making sense of your losses, whether they're ambiguous or clear. May you discover that while your loss is not normal, your grief may be, and that you can live a joyful life even without closure.

Much of this book was written in 2020 but finished in 2021. Over that time, there were numerous spikes in the numbers of sick and dead as the COVID-19 virus covered the world and then mutated. There were also other tragedies, including the death of my husband in the autumn of 2020 from a stroke. He had been ill for some time, but I thought we had more time left together. I did not think I should hide this personal loss from you, as I was often grieving as I wrote. I finished writing just as joyful news came about vaccines. At the same time, masks and social distancing became violent political issues. Tensions grew, and politics became deadly on January 6, 2021, as a mob, incited by an ambiguously lost president, stormed the U.S. Capitol. Yet most people in America were lawful and voted in unprecedented numbers. They adapted to comply with recommendations from scientists and doctors. When a collective response is needed to save lives, tempering our need for individual rights is a sign of resilience.

No doubt, there will be other times of loss and suffering in our lives, hopefully not as massive as during the pandemic. We have been tested in an extraordinary way. May you find the resilience to search for meaning instead of closure, and may you find peace in the sadness of your own losses.

THE MYTH OF CLOSURE

PART ONE

WHAT JUST HAPPENED?

CHAPTER 1

AMBIGUOUS LOSS

Now I've learned, the hard way, that some
poems don't rhyme, and some stories don't have
a clear beginning, middle, or end. . . .
      —Gilda Radner, *It's Always Something*

Neither ambiguity nor loss are popular topics in our culture, but now, due to the pandemic, we're immersed in both. Ambiguous loss is a loss that remains unclear and without official verification or immediate resolution, which may never be achieved. The people we love can be physically gone but kept psychologically present—or the opposite, physically present but psychologically gone. We feel our grief, but because no death has occurred or been verified, it is often criticized as premature. Ambiguous losses then lead to a disenfranchised grief because others do not see the loss as credible and worthy of grief.

Inevitably, such ambiguous losses occur over one's lifetime. For me, as a child, it was the homesickness of my immigrant elders; in my 40s, it was a divorce plus the growing frailty of my formerly strong parents. Now in my 80s, it's the gradual loss of dear friends and family members due to terminal illnesses, including the psychological absence of those who have Alzheimer's disease—or one of the many other illnesses or conditions that cause dementia. And now, what just happened is a pandemic, on a scale few of us have ever experienced before.

This worldwide health crisis brought many ambiguous losses. Loved ones died alone in hospitals with no family allowed, all losing the comfort of a last goodbye; students lost rituals of graduation and saying goodbye to classmates, as well as the chance to meet new friends at the beginning of a new academic year; younger children were schooled at home, many alone in their rooms in front of a computer; others struggled because they had no broadband, computer, or internet access. The critical experiences that traditionally marked growing up were lost—a surreal experience for the young as well as their parents.

Regardless of age, however, we all lost the freedom and independence to move about as we pleased. This had been one of the joys of life, but now we were quarantined. Many lost their jobs or had to work from home; many others lost the security of having health care, enough food for the family, or a roof over their heads. As the pandemic sickened and killed more each day, the uncertainty grew, and we suffered the ultimate loss: the loss of trust in the world as a safe and predictable place. This is the crucible for high anxiety and distress.

To more easily cope and manage the stress of loss, we must first identify what was lost. Below is a list of pandemic losses that many say they have had or are still having. Some of the losses are clear (loss of income, loss of home) and others are ambiguous (loss of trust in the world as a safe place; not knowing where a loved one's remains are). Think about or circle the following that apply to you; if your losses are not listed, you can add them to the end of the appropriate list.

Ambiguous Losses Due to COVID-19

- Loss of hopes, dreams, and plans for your future—the loss of a way of life that had promised fulfillment and satisfaction
- Loss of certainty about safety and health for yourself and family
- Loss of routines
- Loss of playdates for young children and at-school learning for all students regardless of age
- Loss of parental time and freedom to go to work due to the need for at-home schooling for their children
- Loss of ability to be with a loved one who is hospitalized and/or dying
- Loss of traditional rituals of mourning and burial, not knowing where the body of a loved one is
- Loss of ability to celebrate or mourn major life events—births, graduations, marriages, deaths, etc., in community with others

- Loss of support and comfort from your community at times of loss
- Loss of being able to say goodbye to friends as schools and colleges closed abruptly
- Loss of ability to attend large events—concerts, sports, lectures, reunions, and so on
- Loss of control of how much time is spent with partner and children (too much, too little)
- Loss of trust in the world as a fair and just place
- Loss of trust in leaders and authorities
- Loss of freedom to move about as we please
- Loss of . . . (add your own)

Clearer Losses That May Still Have Some Ambiguity and Uncertainty

- Validated deaths of family, friends, colleagues
- Loss of a job
- Loss of a business
- Loss of income
- Loss of retirement savings
- Loss of one's home or apartment
- Loss of security about food and shelter
- Loss of . . . (add your own)

Ambiguous losses are ubiquitous but rarely acknowledged because they are difficult to see, even by those of us experiencing them. While all loss is stressful, ambiguous loss adds additional stress because both the loss and grief are frozen.

All too often then, people simply wait for things to get back to normal, for the loss to be recovered. Sadly, that rarely happens.

To lower your stress now, as the pandemic shifts, identify and acknowledge what you have lost, whether clear or ambiguous, and allow yourself the time and space to grieve those losses. They may not all be about death. During the worst of the pandemic, when you had to work at home and also teach your children, or when you tried to work amid the commotion caused by a family sequestered too long, you needed to grieve the loss of your freedom and independence. Ordinarily, you might have escaped to an office or a coffee shop to work, but those options were also lost during the lockdowns. Most of us lost even the freedom to calm ourselves in the ways we previously did—lunching with friends, going to the gym or yoga studio, golfing, running, getting a massage, or simply knowing we were safe and secure.

More dangerous, though, are ambiguous losses that become traumatic—the loss of loved ones you can't see, the loss of your own health, your home, your job, your business, or enough food to feed your family. The trauma results from the ambiguity that freezes grief and takes away your power to function. Feeling stuck, worthless, overwhelmed, and without hope is dangerous to your health. If such losses make you feel helpless, hopeless, or self-loathing, seek professional therapy. Doing so can save your life.

If you are sure you don't need professional help, what can you do to help yourself? *First*, to lower your stress and anxiety during confusing times, increase your tolerance for ambiguity. This is not an easy task in a can-do culture, but necessary for building the resilience to withstand stress. This is best done in the company of others who can challenge your thinking. *Second*, with so many unanswered questions about the virus and vaccines, jobs and schools, wearing masks or not, and adapting to being quarantined, we need to be aware that our anxiety was and is not a psychiatric disorder. Said another way, our anxiety during the pandemic was likely a normal response to an abnormal situation. It was born out of the ambiguity that surrounded our losses—the not knowing, the lack of factual information, the confusion and doubt about what was happening, if and when it would be over, and what to do to stay safe. To live more calmly now, we not only increase our tolerance for ambiguity but view the culprit as outside of ourselves. It is not our fault. Surely, the pandemic qualified as an abnormal situation, so it helps to know that the source of our anxiety during that time came from a context of actual danger and not from our personal frailty. *Third*, while we may pride ourselves on rugged individualism, we also need to think more about others. Wearing a mask is not a political issue; it's about protecting the community and those we love. We are in this pandemic together and now we can rebuild together.

To understand what just happened and what is still happening as a result of COVID-19, I focus on the stress of loss and the resilience needed to tolerate its ambiguity for the long haul. This focus on stress and resilience is not meant to negate medical approaches but is offered to augment the increasing attention to disease and disorder. I offer no cure, but hopefully more understanding of the nuances of loss, so that you can strengthen your resilience to weather these times of uncertainty and change.

How Do We Manage the Stress of Ambiguous Loss? The Work Begins

No matter where I work, here or abroad, with survivors of war, tsunami, terrorism—and yes, diseases that have no cure—here's how I always begin with an individual, family, or community group: "What you are experiencing is ambiguous loss; it is the most difficult loss because it defies resolution. This is not your fault. The problem is the ambiguity, not you. It can traumatize." With this, the work begins.

Types of Ambiguous Loss

There are two types of ambiguous loss. The first is physical—no body to bury, no proof of death. We see this now with COVID-19 deaths where families are not allowed to view the body or have the usual funeral rituals of mourning and burial. After the 9/11 attack on the Twin Towers in New York City and after the tsunami in Fukushima in Japan in 2011, families also suffered from physical ambiguous loss. About 40% of the families of those still missing from 9/11 have no proof of death and are left holding the ambiguity of loss. During the pandemic, many lost the age-old opportunity to be with loved ones as they are dying, leading to a physical ambiguous loss that many will not forget.

In addition to these catastrophic events, there are also everyday examples of physical ambiguous loss—breakups, separations, divorce, migration and immigration—and the loss of job security of close to a million mothers who quit their paid employment to take care of their children once schools and day care centers closed due to the coronavirus. Whether or not these women will regain the security of a job remains unclear.

Today, I add "ghosting" to this list of more common physical ambiguous losses, meaning that someone suddenly cuts you off, vanishing from your life with no further communication or contact. Intentionally causing such an ambiguous loss is a cruel way to end a relationship. With no way to know that the breakup is permanent, the person left behind is held in a limbo of uncertainty and is unable to find enough meaning to move forward in life. Without a clear goodbye, they are more likely to keep hoping the lost person will return and thus may not get on with their lives in a new way.

The second type of ambiguous loss is psychological. A loved one is physically present but psychologically absent; here in body but gone in mind—as with dementia and traumatic brain injuries, or serious mental illnesses, including clinical depression. More common examples of being physically present but psychologically absent are obsessions or preoccupations with social media, gaming, or constantly checking one's phone. During the pandemic, however, many of us were preoccupied with worry and anxiety about the virus, and obsessed with washing our hands, wiping down groceries and mail, and distrusting others who got too close. In normal times, these behaviors would likely have been viewed as obsessive and causing psychological ambiguous loss, but during the pandemic, they were necessary to stay safe.

Experiencing Both Types of Ambiguous Loss at the Same Time

An important note: We can have both types of ambiguous loss at one time. For example, a mother whose husband disappeared—a physical type of ambiguous loss—also becomes clinically depressed. Now, her children feel they have lost both parents. Mom is physically present but absent emotionally, due to her depression. And Dad is physically gone. The children in this case are experiencing both types of ambiguous loss at the same time. After 9/11 in New York City, as well as in Japan after the tsunami, we saw this situation of dual parental losses all too often.

Multiple Ambiguous Losses of Either Type at the Same Time

Another note: We can experience multiple ambiguous losses at the same time. For example, a man who has a wife with advanced dementia and a son who is addicted to drugs is simultaneously enduring two psychological ambiguous losses. He feels as if he has lost both, but both are still with him at home. For his wife, there is likely no chance of coming back, but he continues to hope that his son will go into treatment and come back. For now, however, neither is emotionally present for him.

New Information About Ambiguous Loss

Since the pandemic began, and requests for interviews about ambiguous loss spiked, I have done some new thinking. Originally, as a family therapist, I saw ambiguous loss as primarily a family matter. A person in the family was missing, and the remaining members experienced ambiguous loss. In the 1970s and '80s, I studied families of missing pilots (Type 1 ambiguous loss) and in the 1990s, families of veterans who had Alzheimer's disease (Type 2 ambiguous loss). Back then, I saw ambiguous loss as the rupture of a close relationship with a family member who was lost either physically or psychologically, in either body or mind. Now, after much thinking since that fateful Memorial Day when George Floyd was killed, here in my hometown of Minneapolis, combined with the questions coming to me from around the world, I have expanded my ideas about ambiguous loss. It can happen to one person, one family, a local community, or the global community.

Personal Ambiguous Loss (Internally Caused)

Personal ambiguous loss happens when we lose something that affects our relationship to ourselves—no longer being as we used to be or who we were, physically and psychologically. We are still living but aware that we have lost a part of our body or mind. Physically, a soldier loses their leg and is no longer able to serve or be the athlete they were; a person has cancer that requires removal of their reproductive organs and can no longer have the children they wanted; psychologically, a brilliant teacher loses their memory and can no longer teach; or a football player now has chronic traumatic encephalopathy from repeated head injuries and can no longer play. Or it could be simply ourselves, growing older and losing many of the assets and capacities we had when we were young. Whether such personal losses are physical or psychological, the confusion about what we have lost and who we are now is disturbing. Something about us has disappeared, and we know it. This requires some grieving, ideally not alone.

Personal Ambiguous Loss (Externally Caused)

So far, I have used examples of personal ambiguous loss that is caused by some loss *inside* a person's body or mind—the loss of one's eyesight, hearing, voice, or memory. But personal ambiguous loss can also come from an external societal source. For example, a person has COVID-19 and is stigmatized by their community; or a physician who was successful and respected in another country must now drive a cab in this country because he does not have the right license. Or today, due to the external force of a deadly virus, many people have lost status as homeowners or business owners. What this tells me is that ambiguous loss, at the personal or family levels, has many nuances. And now, at this troubled time, there is still more to consider.

Ambiguous Loss at the Societal and Global Levels

Since the pandemic, my new thinking about ambiguous loss has gone even beyond nuances in individual and family levels to a societal and even global application of this lens. Since COVID-19 hit, we saw the murder of George Floyd recorded on video by a teenaged girl on the way to the grocery store. While this murder took place in Minneapolis, the world saw what she filmed, and it brought to light again centuries-old anger and grief from the Black community and others—the unresolved cruelty and losses from slavery and the systemic racism that is still with us today. I received a flood of inquiries about whether such societal losses were ambiguous losses. My answer was yes. Losses never acknowledged remain ambiguous and unresolved, so the trauma is passed down across the generations and can erupt years later.

This broader application of societal ambiguous loss adds yet more nuances—for losses that occur to a larger society, in this case, centuries ago but never acknowledged or resolved. I think of those whom the larger societies or people in power deemed less worthy, who were persecuted for their beliefs or sold off or unjustly singled out for their skin color. It will be up to a new generation of researchers and clinicians to determine if, through the lens of ambiguous loss, those losses will be acknowledged and reckoned with through societal change. Whatever helps us to better understand the pain of past losses can lead us to more empathy and societal change.

To work at this societal level, we must first acknowledge that in many countries, mastery and control are imperatives. But when we are faced with a problem that has no solution, or no immediate solution (like the pandemic), we become distraught and anxious or angry, and are less able to cope than people in cultures more focused on community. Feeling we can solve anything works well most of the time, but when a problem has no solution, when a loved one disappears without a trace or has an illness that has no cure, the mastery-oriented way of thinking is not helpful. The ambiguous loss approach requires a new way of thinking that is more useful in times of uncertainty—like now.

Indeed, people are asking me for still more clarification. They tell me they think the losses from climate change are ambiguous losses and ask if I agree. I do. The losses resulting from melting ice caps, higher oceanic levels, the disappearance of forests and fertile lands to grow food are not yet acknowledged by everyone, but life threatening to all. Things critical for human life are going missing—clean air, clean water, food, safety from violent storms. The lens of ambiguous loss can help us make sense of these contemporary losses so that interventions can take place at multiple levels—the personal, the familial, the societal, and the global.

These multilevel ambiguous losses are occurring right now and increasing the population's anxiety as well as anger. The challenge, however, can also strengthen our resilience—if we learn to think less about mastery and our own agency and more about empathy and concern for others. Once we face the realities of loss, ours and those of our neighbors, we see the necessity for change, for what is called a paradigm shift. We have had those before, at the turn of the century when women marched for the right to vote, and in the 1960s and '70s when people marched for civil rights and withdrawal from the Vietnam War. In the decades that followed, there were many demonstrations for rights: equality for gender and sexual minorities, for the differently abled, for social justice against racism. And, sadly, still for the ability to vote. Along with climate change and a deadly pandemic, all are part of the context in which we find ourselves now. Change is afoot; if we are to survive, we must change our way of thinking about loss—and its ambiguity. Eventually, it finds us. We can't have certainty all the time.

CHAPTER 2

THE MYTH OF CLOSURE

Death ends a life, not a relationship.
—Mitch Albom, *Tuesdays with Morrie*

A s the pandemic raged on, losses of all kinds were piling up for people. The barber down the street, a family man, lost his business; a prominent restaurateur lost his restaurant; and dozens of smaller eateries and shops have shut their doors. The term "closure" was heard routinely as the pandemic closed many small businesses, many forever. While the term fits for describing businesses that close their doors, closure does not fit the experience of losing someone we love.

In the popular vernacular, closure is unfortunately used to describe the ending of the grief that comes after loss. The assumption is that you'll be "over it," done with your sorrow once you have closure. Not true. When Mitch Albom writes about death not ending a relationship, he knows that his visits with Morrie every Tuesday formed a bond that continues even after death. There is no closure, nor does there need to be.

As a family therapist, I worked primarily with people suffering from unexpected and traumatic losses, most of them full of ambiguity. What I learned is that even with the most extreme cases of loss, having no closure does not have to be devastating.

Sarah was a traumatized 19-year-old woman who was the survivor of a horrific small plane crash that killed her father and brother and left her mother with third-degree burns. It's been over a decade now since we ended our therapy work together. She completed her bachelor's degree with honors, married, had two children, then finished her master's degree, and moved with her husband and children across the country to work as a marriage and family therapist. On the tenth anniversary of her losses, she wrote to me:

> When I lost Dad and Zachary, the pain and suffering from the experience forced me to stare at the closed door. I couldn't believe what had happened; there were still conflicts between my father and me, and the disbelief that my brother was gone was too overwhelming. . . . However, as the ten-year anniversary approaches, I am grateful that the energy that flows between us continues, not on a physical level, but now as a highly emotional and spiritual experience. These relationships have actually continued to evolve, especially with my father. Forgiveness has occurred

between my father and me and acceptance that my brother was killed at such a young age happened. Forgiveness and acceptance. These two acts have expanded my heart in ways that I could not possibly imagine. I now have the ability to empathize with others who are suffering and genuinely be in the moment with them. People ask, "Have you found closure in their deaths?" Honestly, no. However, I have accepted what was—what has happened, and what will be. Because in the end, I actually have NO control over other people's destinies, but I can continue to accept and grow in mine.

And then there is Donna. Her loss was, and still is, more ambiguous. In 2007, her husband vanished at sea. He has not been seen since, nor was any debris from his red sailboat found. Donna has struggled deeply with the ambiguity of this loss and now, 14 years later, is enjoying her life in a new way. She moved back to her hometown, a city in the Midwest, and returned to her early talent of writing poetry. She also wrote about closure and the hurt it causes: "People wanted to call me a 'widow' right after he disappeared. . . . They would say, 'Oh, Donna, just call yourself a widow. It will make your life easier and no one will know the difference . . . '", except, she said, she would know the difference. It is not unusual for others to want closure more than the person experiencing the loss.

Donna continued, "To call myself a widow was diminishing my life experience. It was another way of tucking away what happened under the cultural veneer of a *closure* word." Later she wrote:

> *People are often so uncomfortable being in the room with loss. With strangers, I am very careful not to mention the word "disappeared," for all sorts of reasons, including not wanting to see their discomfort about my missing husband or go into the world of voyeurism with them. Alzheimer's is handled a bit easier, I think, because of its frequency now, but even so, there is a "hush" in the room when it is discussed, as though if we talk in a hush about this loss of a living person, it might be less horrible. It might not happen to us.*

It was from people like Donna and Sarah that I learned again and again that closure is a myth. I saw repeatedly that keeping loved ones present in one's heart and mind, even after they have disappeared or died, helps one to hold the loss and its grief without seeking an absolute ending. Yes, they accept the loss as real and, at the same time, move forward with new hopes. They take a risk to change and do not wait for things to go back to the way they were. Instead of seeking closure, they find ways to hold the ambiguity and live with it.

For Sarah, while referring to her father and brother as "a part of my soul that will remain for eternity," her story gradually changed over the years from one of immense trauma and loss to one of higher purpose—raising her own children now in a healthier environment than she experienced and honoring her deceased father, who always wanted her to go to college, by becoming a licensed family therapist who can help others.

Donna found meaning in more artistic ways, becoming an accomplished poet, making friends in the arts community, and becoming a wise and compassionate head of her extended family. Neither Donna nor Sarah believes today that closure is possible or essential. They are both at peace with a "continuing bond." Donna may wish for more certainty, but that has not stopped her from living life in all of its fullness.

■ ■ ■

While closure is a frequently used term, what does it mean? Sociologist Nancy Berns analyzed the term and found that there was no agreed-upon answer among the people who use it. In her study, closure was described as:

> *justice, peace, healing, acceptance, forgiveness, moving on, resolution, answered questions, or revenge. And how are you supposed to find this closure? People try to find closure by planting trees, acquiring memorial tattoos, forgiving murderers, watching killers die, talking to offenders, writing letters, burning letters, burning wedding dresses, burying wedding rings, casting spells, taking trips to Hawaii, buying expensive pet urns, committing suicide, talking to dead people, reviewing autopsies, and planning funerals.*

And she tells us this is just a partial list.

My definition of closure, however, focuses on the meaning of the word itself. In relation to loss, closure means termination, finality, something finished. It implies a clear and absolute ending. However, many people don't want such total, absolute termination of a relationship. As referred to earlier, Mitch Albom wrote, "Death ends a life, not a relationship." I add that while divorce ends a marriage, it does not always have to end a friendship and coparenting.

When I was in graduate school in Madison, family therapist Carl Whitaker angered some of us in his seminar when he blithely said, "You can never get divorced." I had just gotten divorced, and that was not what I wanted to hear. I wanted closure and thought the divorce decree was the end of it. But after some years passed, I noticed my empathy for my ex-husband had grown. I now knew what Whitaker meant. Once there has been an attachment, even a legal divorce might not end the relationship. Still today, I think kindly of that husband of my youth when I see his good looks and athleticism in both of my children.

In the end, the cost of seeking closure is that it's impossible and thus saps our energy and distracts us from seeing other coping options that could lead to more emotional growth and resilience. The benefits of not seeking closure are many: *First*, it allows us to savor or resist the parts of ourselves that others have influenced, positively or negatively; *second*, giving up on closure increases our tolerance for ambiguity and thus makes us more resilient for future experiences of loss; *third*, without needing closure, we can feel more rooted in this world because we now see more than just ourselves in it. We are genetically part of those who have gone before us—and thus part of the human species. With continuity instead of closure, we are not alone.

In my view then, the idea of closure cuts off these real and symbolic connections and thus often hurts those left behind. Berns said that after giving birth to her stillborn son, people encouraged her to move on from her grief—or assumed she had already done so. This is when she first became wary of the term and also of businesses and politicians who use closure to sell products and agendas. Nevertheless, although it's hurtful, many still use the term. Even the "proof" of an official death certificate may not suffice for what some think of as closure.

For example, with the many killings of Black people still today, families are told they will have closure when the judge sentences the perpetrator to their satisfaction. But this is an illusion. Yes, there is the closure of the trial or the legal case, but there is no closure for the relationship the family lost. While people often say they need justice to have closure, this may be a misnomer, the wrong word. I imagine that what they want—and deserve—is justice, to have the certainty of systemic change so that other families do not have to bear the same pain. Shutting the door on the memory of the person they lost is not their goal.

■ ■ ■

What about the many other losses during this time of loss and change? Will the barber who lost his shop find closure on his losses once the pandemic is over? I doubt that. Will the millions worldwide who lost family members to the virus find closure once the virus is controlled? I doubt that too and do not encourage anyone to wait for it. Instead, we should search for meaning and purpose in our lives after this horrific time in history.

For me, one of those new meanings is that I now understand more deeply that my Swiss immigrant family on a
tenant farm in Wisconsin pulled ourselves up by the boot-
straps during the Great Depression more easily because of
white privilege. While my family was poor and spoke with
heavy accents, I had more opportunities. I also need to educate myself more now about people who still live from paycheck to paycheck. I did that, too, once, but have not paid
attention to current numbers. And while I have received
many speeding tickets in my day, and sometimes talked back
to the police officer, I need to educate myself again about
white privilege and the injustices still being perpetrated by
police against Black people. In the twilight of my life, this
time of pandemic has opened my eyes to the huge disparities
in health care, housing, food availability, and opportunities
for education, employment, housing, and thus income. My
stunted awareness was likely awakened because the pandemic made me slow down enough to *see* and *hear* all that
was happening.

Millions have been sickened by or died from the coronavirus. Rather than seeking closure on this terrible time, let's
face the enormity of the losses, grieve, support others who
are grieving, and find a way to help bring about systemic
change.

To all of you who are grieving someone or something you
loved and lost during this pandemic, may I say this: What
you have lost is not the chance for closure, but more likely,
the chance to say goodbye, to be with your loved one as they
lay dying, to finish unfinished business, to ask for or give

forgiveness, to say, "I love you" and to touch your loved one's hand for the last time. It is not closure you need but certainty that your loved one is gone, that they understood why you could not be there to comfort them, that they loved you and forgave you in their last moments of life. Without these things, some doubts may linger for you, but that is the nature of loss. Its ending is never perfect even in the best of times.

Whether our losses are human or material, concrete or ambiguous, we will not forget this plague. At every class reunion, the kids who never had a graduation ceremony will remember the pandemic; health care workers will forever remember the patients they lost; businesspeople will remember the customers and money lost; employees will remember the jobs and income lost; and parents will remember the loss of having their kids learning at home, instead of with others in school, as they always have. Even homes were lost due to deadly hurricanes, floods, and wildfires that came during the pandemic. There will be no closure on this hellish time; it will leave its mark on all of us, and like the Great Depression and World War II, will shape an entire generation.

CHAPTER 3

RACISM AS UNRESOLVED LOSS

The world needed to see what I was seeing. Stuff like this happens in silence too many times.
—Darnella Frazier

A s a family therapist, I have always been interested in the systemic workings of families. My first studies of ambiguous loss focused on military couples—one gone missing, the other left behind. For research purposes, I interviewed the wives of pilots classified as MIA (missing in action). But for therapy interventions, I worked with them in the context of their whole families—and they defined who their family was. I wanted their self-defined family because they needed the people who were supporting them to come with them to the sessions. Sometimes, it was biological relatives, sometimes a neighbor or friend who came with them, and sometimes it was their pastor. Whether it was for family members of veterans with Alzheimer's disease or workers missing after 9/11, or people in my clinical practice, working within their systemic context proved useful and supportive to them. The people with missing loved ones had someone they could go home with after our work together. But there is another tool that family therapists use—family of origin work. We saw that patterns of coping, resilience, and trauma often occurred across the generations. For this reason, we found it useful in therapy to trace family patterns of trauma and resilience back to former generations. Doing this helped people understand more fully their family history and how they might cope more effectively with present losses.

Today, in our national family, there are still unresolved losses from racial injustices, present and past. Based on our history of the dead and missing from the Civil War, genocide, and slavery of people of color, we are indeed a "republic of suffering." But we are also a nation of frozen grief and trauma resulting from families having had loved ones go missing or disappear. We are a nation born out of ambiguous losses, still carrying the anger and grief that lingers. It is a time now for a reckoning.

With the slavery of African Americans, as well as genocide, uprooting, and residential schools for Native Americans, family members were brutally separated, torn apart from one another. Family relationships were ruptured: paternal parentage was often unclear; children were sold away from their mothers; couples who wanted to be married were split apart on the auction block. With slavery, the right to have a family life was lost. Given this messy history of ambiguous losses, no wonder our society has valued the tidiness of closure.

Of course, closure never happened. The generations who

descended from slavery have not forgotten. Even the loss of the Civil War has had no closure.

In addition to the monumental problem of the COVID-19 pandemic and its many deaths, systemic racism became clearer to many of us during this same period. First there was the murder of George Floyd on May 25, 2020, then the video of his death that went around the world, then Black Lives Matter marches, and some riots; and then, on January 6, 2021, thousands of white supremacists, fired up by presidential mendacity, stormed our nation's capital, carrying a Confederate flag into the Capitol building, threatening to kill lawmakers, and causing death and mayhem. Watching this on television, I was stunned. I saw more clearly than ever before that white supremacy still remains a major threat to our nation today. As a result, the stress and trauma suffered by Black people as well as all people of color continue today. Until we all see that problem, our national family cannot heal. To acknowledge the trauma from the terrible losses caused by slavery, we must first look back to understand the problem, and only then can we look forward to new changes and systemic solutions.

Historically, while many witnessed the unjust deaths of loved ones, I focus here on the losses that remain unclear. What were the ambiguous losses of slavery? Being kidnapped from family and homeland, chained into a slave ship, and sold at auction for a lifetime of brutal bondage, denied marriage and family; losing the sense of control over your life, your loved ones, your body, your agency, your self-esteem. Not all were actual deaths, but all were immensely traumatic losses. Women were raped and traumatized during their pregnancies.

Children were sold away from their mothers on the auction block. Families were intentionally broken apart. There is no closure for such horrific losses. Nor should there be. Their pain is remembered today in the bodies and minds of their descendants, but also for those of us without that history, in books, films, and programs like *Finding Your Roots*, all of which reveal some of those family patterns of suffering and also resilience.

A former slave, Henry Bibb, who experienced and survived that traumatic life, and then escaped to Canada and became a newspaperman, tells his story:

> *I was taken away from my mother, and hired out to labor for various persons, eight or ten years in succession; and all my wages were expended for the education of Harriet White, my playmate. It was then my sorrows and sufferings commenced. It was then I first commenced seeing and feeling that I was a wretched slave, compelled to work under the lash without wages, and often without clothes enough to hide my nakedness. I have often worked without half enough to eat, both late and early, by day and by night. I have often laid my wearied limbs down at night to rest upon a dirt floor, or a bench, without any covering at all, because I had nowhere else to rest my wearied body, after having worked hard all the day. I have also been compelled in early life, to go at the bidding of a tyrant, through all kinds of weather, hot or cold, wet or dry, and without shoes frequently, until the month of December, with my bare feet on the cold frosty ground, cracked open and bleeding as I walked. Reader, believe me when I say, that no tongue, nor pen ever has or can express*

the horrors of American Slavery. Consequently, I despair in finding language to express adequately the deep feeling of my soul, as I contemplate the past history of my life.

From the loss of his mother and her nurturance to loss of basic resources of food, clothing, shelter, and with a childhood full of heavy work, young Henry was already overloaded with the stress and trauma of ambiguous loss. Does such historical trauma still affect Black families today? Fortunately, researchers are working to answer this question.

The Cross-Generational Transmission of Trauma

While people interested in finding their roots and origins have felt that patterns of coping and resilience were passed down across the generations through the nurturance of children and their observations, there is now growing scientific evidence that cross-generational transmission of trauma does indeed occur. But there are differing views about *how* this happens. Is this a biological process? Or is it a social process? Is it nature or nurture? Likely, it is both.

On the biological side, inheritance of the effects of trauma is of key interest in epigenetics, the study of inheritable changes in DNA that change its expression, but not the gene itself. We know from past studies of Holocaust mothers and their children that the effects of trauma can be passed down from mother to child. Clinician and researcher Bessel van der Kolk also finds that past trauma affects our bodies. Research on whether such biological changes have affected African Americans through the generations in the same way is ongoing.

Meanwhile, from a more social-psychological perspective, Joy DeGruy proposes a theory of post-traumatic slave syndrome. Indeed, many people of color, old and young, regularly experience traumatic loss and stress, so I offer some cautions about the original term "post-traumatic stress disorder" (PTSD). First, the word "post" negates the ongoing losses that are still traumatizing Black lives today. Their burden is not just post-traumatic; it is current. Second, I am wary of adapting mental illness terms (such as "disorder" or "syndrome") for people who have been traumatized by an outside force. Most Black people were not deficient in mental health. In fact, they were exceptionally resilient. They did not choose to be captured as slaves; nor did they choose to give up their freedom and submit to others. Choice is a privilege that anyone who has been indentured, raped, wounded, captured, or abused does not have.

As with other kinds of ambiguous losses, the source of trauma emerges from a person's external context, and not from within their psyche. Using a term similar to PTSD may result in an expectation for Black people to change more than society should. While cross-generational transmission of trauma is real, using medical terms might unintentionally lead to blaming the victim.

Hopefully, current scientists and scholars will study not just the problems of loss and trauma, but also the cross-generational transmission of resilience. Resilience exists today, and it existed in the past, as Henry Bibb, a former slave, continues his story of survival:

Although I have suffered much from the lash, and for want of food and raiment; I confess that it was no disadvantage to be passed through the hands of so many families, as the only source of information that I had to enlighten my mind, consisted in what I could see and hear from others. Slaves were not allowed books, pen, ink, nor paper, to improve their minds. But it seems to me now, that I was particularly observing, and apt to retain what came under my observation. But more especially, all that I heard about liberty and freedom to the slaves, I never forgot. Among other good trades I learned the art of running away to perfection. I made a regular business of it, and never gave it up, until I had broken the bands of slavery, and landed myself safely in Canada, where I was regarded as a man, and not as a thing.

Many African Americans continue to find strength and resilience in the ways their ancestors did—through belief in God, songs of hope and overcoming, prayer, community, and valuing the extended family. And in the way Henry Bibb did, with perseverance, intelligence, and learning a trade. While traumatic loss still happens today, we can see resilience as well—if we look for it.

Racism Seen Around the World

On Memorial Day, 2020, in Minneapolis, 17-year-old Darnella Frazier was taking her nine-year-old cousin to their neighborhood grocery store when she saw some police officers scuffling with a tall Black man who was often in that neighborhood. His name was George Floyd. She pulled out her cell phone and began recording. He was now on the pavement with a white policeman's knee on his neck. Darnella was only five feet away from that policeman, and he was glaring at her. But she kept filming. Many times, Mr. Floyd said he couldn't breathe. She repeated it for the police to make sure they heard it. Bystanders were yelling for the policeman to let him breathe. Barely audible, George Floyd pleaded, "Mama, Mama, Mama." A few minutes later, he was quiet. He died. The policeman's knee had been on his neck for over nine minutes.

This courageous young woman's video was seen around the world and opened the eyes of millions of people, including me. I had not seen clearly enough before that unjust killings of Black people still continue at an alarming rate today. Black lives have not always mattered. And they must. Our nation's legacy of unresolved loss must not be closed off. It is painful to face, but closing the door on either past or present traumatic losses will delay the reckonings needed to heal and move forward. Closing our eyes to the problem is not the answer. Once we see the problems of this time more clearly, we can work on changes, and our national family can begin healing.

My Early Learning

I am not an expert on the Black experience, but a learner. My colleague in family therapy, Elaine Pinderhughes, was one of the first to teach me that historical context matters for human development and that being traumatized instead of nurtured will affect not only children but also their own off-spring as well. She wrote that continued losses and repeated trauma had been, since slavery, part of the experience of African Americans in the United States. As a family thera-pist, she wrote that "as a consequence of their 400 years of entrapment in racism," their losses were "nothing short of cataclysmic." More than forty years ago, she wrote about the effects of lynchings, riots, murders, cross burnings, and the psychic numbing and sense of hopelessness that resulted, limiting one's personal adaptability to whatever comes next. Overall, the context in which early African Americans were forced to live has affected future generations.

Post-slavery conditions were not good either. There were the unjust events of the Reconstruction Period, family losses due to Northern migration, and the deindustrialization due to technology. As ongoing inequities continued to keep Black families in poverty, and while white immigrants were pre-ferred over Blacks for employment, the poverty of Black workers was extended across the generations. During the 1960s to the 1980s, blue-collar jobs were stable in the facto-ries of the North, but racial inequities still existed and these factory jobs eventually gave way to technology, which broke up many Black families.

Finally, Elaine Pinderhughes made one other point that I never forgot and want to emphasize today. She wrote, "It is unethical and irresponsible to medicate and therapize a population suffering from such long-standing vulnerability without also removing its source. This means that white America must give up the benefits of racism."

Hard words to hear. There is much more then to learn, not about the problem—we know what that is now—but about how to end such systemic racism so that we can be a more equitable and compassionate human family.

PART TWO

STAYING STRONG AND RESILIENT

CHAPTER 4

RESILIENCE: OUR BEST HOPE IN THE FACE OF AMBIGUOUS LOSS

*Do not judge me by my successes, judge me by how
many times I fell down and got back up again.*
—Nelson Mandela

In New York City, after the September 11, 2001, terrorist attacks on the Twin Towers of the World Trade Center, only one tree was left standing near the site. After near devastation, it is now flourishing as the Survivor Tree at the 9/11 Memorial. In Washington, DC's National Arboretum, there is a mushroom-shaped tree, 390 years old, that was donated by Japan to the arboretum in 1976. The surprise of resilience is that this ancient bonsai tree survived the atomic bomb blast in Hiroshima during World War II. It stands as a symbol of resilience. In Fukushima, Japan, after the tsunami of March

10, 2011, I saw a lone tree remaining on the beach. Because it withstood the force of the waters, the people considered it a symbol of resilience. These trees that survived against all odds, against monumental forces, have become symbols of resilience for people. The trees that survive give them hope.

Resilience in human beings is metaphorically similar to that of the surviving trees. If we survive an onslaught of high stress or trauma, and we remain flexible and bounce back to carry on, then we too can grow stronger after such devasting pressure. We not only survive but gain strength from the challenge.

Resilience, then, is defined as the ability to be flexible in the face of pressure without breaking down. Resilient people have the capacity to bounce back after stress to a level of functioning even higher than before that stress occurred. The assumption is that we learn something from the stress we experience and thus become stronger for it. In my work, I found resilient individuals as well as families and communities.

While resilience is valued, I nevertheless need to clarify some cautions about it:

1. There are racial and cultural differences in how people define and achieve resilience. Social worker Hollingsworth writes that "when resilience is defined as being confronted with adversity and surviving and prospering in spite of it, there certainly is evidence of it in Black families." I agree. Given the racism, discrimination, and oppression they have experienced, they are a resilient people.

2. Focusing too much on resilience may blind us to the need to prevent or fix the problems that caused the trauma—for example, poverty, racism, abuse, war, rape, or homelessness, kidnapping, femicide.

3. The singular focus on resilience is justified only when the distress causing the problem is unavoidable. That is, while the first studies on resilience were done with poor and homeless children in Hawaii, the problems of homelessness and poverty are avoidable. They can be ameliorated.

4. While building resilience is not always the right answer, it is, however, especially needed for a problem that has no immediate solution. It can go on and on, even for a lifetime. One example is ambiguous loss. With long-term ambiguous losses, resilience requires even more than flexibility and recovery to a level higher than before. It requires a tolerance for ambiguity. For example, during the stress of a catastrophe, people who need certainty and immediate answers may be more brittle than flexible, thus more likely to give up or break down—unlike the survivor trees.

5. Family and community can both be sources of resilience—and barriers to it. A supportive and nurturing family is ideal for building resilience; a family that neglects or abuses its members is not. For example, in some situations, rebellion is better than continuing to bend down with resilience to an abuser. If people have fewer means or less agency, they may have no other choice than to submit and give up. These are the people who must always bend and adapt. They're the ones who live near rivers that

flood or in poor housing that impairs the health of their children. For this reason, we must see resilience as a way we adapt to trouble or scarcity—and not as the systemic solution. In any time of pandemic, the danger of illness can't be avoided, but we can minimize that danger. We can wear a mask. Resilient people can adapt.

During the pandemic, with soaring numbers of deaths plus ambiguous losses, one of the most traumatic was being unable to say goodbye to loved ones who were dying. Also, if you were a first responder or health care worker, you likely lost your feelings of safety as you became afraid that you would inadvertently bring the virus home to your family. There were also the ambiguous losses of the customary markers for life's transitions—birthdays, graduations, weddings, and funerals, all ambiguous losses during the pandemic. Life was greatly altered by a virus that was raging and is now mutating with more virulence. That uncertainty, plus economic and political tensions, cause us to feel helpless and hopeless, so there is still widespread anxiety, sadness, and depression. Because the situation is not yet under control as I write this, resilience is still needed to get us through our daily lives. Here is the good news to give us hope:

1. Resilience is more common than we think. Most people have a self-righting ability to cope. This includes children if they are taught coping skills early on.
2. There are multiple and unexpected pathways to resilience. Thus, there is much diversity in coping skills as

influenced by race, religious beliefs, and culture, as well as gender and age.

3. For children, resilience is often called "ordinary magic," meaning that kids are naturally flexible, and thus good adapters to situations of stress, even those with "substantial challenges." We see children who thrive and become successful adults, even with the stress of ambiguous loss. Because children tend to be more adaptable than adults, traumatized parents or parents fighting with each other are encouraged to seek help for themselves, and not just think it's the children who need help. In Sweden, children who thrive despite adversity are called "dandelion children." A "dandelion child" has the capacity to survive and even thrive in harsh circumstances, whereas an "orchid child" requires more nurturance to flourish.

4. Finally, the good news is that we can build our resilience in multiple ways. For example, we can build resilience by managing the daily hassles of everyday life—getting the kids fed, getting ourselves to work, getting the bills paid, putting food on the table, and keeping things organized. There is also the occasional crisis which, if it doesn't harm us, can strengthen us. The point is that we can increase our resilience for managing stress by grappling with the problems of everyday life. This is also the reason why we should not always rescue children from solving their own problems. If we do this too often, they won't learn how to cope with the stress. While children need to be protected, we also need to give them the opportunity to build their own resilience, sometimes allowing them to figure things out on their own.

Resilience From Community Support

Early in the pandemic, New York intensive care nurses were overwhelmed with the high number of patients needing their care. As virus cases continued to flood into the hospital, an exhausted nurse wondered how they could cope. And then, a group of Utah nurses and doctors offered the New York doctors and nurses desperately needed relief. A New York nurse wondered why someone would come across the country to voluntarily put themselves at risk for COVID-19. "It was a selfless act," she said, "and it meant we were not alone. It gave us the tremendous support we were craving". Then, months later when the virus spiked farther west, this New York nurse and others went to Utah to help.

This is an example of community support increasing the resilience of exhausted nurses and doctors. Knowing that others care about you, and that you are not alone in a crisis, provides the strength needed to stay the course. You catch a second breath; you don't give up, because now, someone has offered their help.

Sometimes your community support groups may even feel like family to you. This is especially true with longtime groups such as the people you work with, sports teams, veteran's groups, neighbors, and religious congregations. We depend on our community support groups for help in a crisis and with recovery. Yet too many people in our communities do not have such support systems around them. They're truly alone. But, we see now during the pandemic people helping people. Not only medical teams, but teachers helping other teachers, parents helping other parents, and neighbors help-ing other neighbors. In times of trouble, we especially need community.

Resilience From a Psychological Family

A psychological family is the family in one's heart and mind. It refers to our personal beliefs about who is in or out of our family. It can include pets, a deity, friends, or people we have never met, such as ancestors, birth parents of an adoptive child, even the imagined fathers who were sperm donors. They may be people who feel to us like a parent, grandparent, brother, sister, uncle, or aunt. They may or may not be physically present in your life, or biologically related, but they are always there in your heart and mind. In time of trouble or celebration, it is this family in your heart and mind that is always with you and can become a support you can draw on anytime, no matter where you are.

Some form of the psychological family exists in all cul-tures, but in different ways. African Americans may still tend to see family flexibly, since fictive kin (persons treated like family but not related by blood or marriage) have his-torically been part of Black culture. During slavery, when parents were sold away, their children left behind were cared for by others in the community, a functional adapta-tion that we still see today. Rather than biology, family was and still can be a group of people who are bonded, referring to one another as sister or brother, indicating a feeling of family.

Today, we also see psychological bonding in chosen family networks, for example, military families, expat families living in foreign countries, and kinship family networks among gender and sexual minorities. They find people who *feel* like family and group together to care for one another, raise the children, and protect each other based on chosen kinship.

In more Eastern cultures, that feeling is often realized through a continuing bond with ancestors. For example, after the 2011 tsunami in northeastern Japan, many survivors were comforted by knowing that their ancestors were now looking after loved ones who were washed away. A Thai family near where I live places a plate of fresh food in the window of their restaurant each day for their ancestors. Westerners, in our ways, may also keep our ancestors psychologically present in our lives. For me, it's the love of the same foods and recipes my ancestors loved, and the music they loved that I still listen to. They're here with me, in my DNA, and also in my memory during good times and bad.

To know who your psychological family is, draw a large circle. Sketch simple figures inside that circle to represent the people you consider family. They can be ancestors, recently deceased, or people present in your life today. They can be related to you by blood or marriage or not at all. A good way to judge who is in your psychological family is to ask yourself who you want to be present, physically or symbolically, at your major life events—graduations, weddings, birthdays, or any other major events you might have. If you have a significant other, or children, compare your drawings. There will be differences, and they are important to acknowledge and accept—especially in divorced or remarried families, step-families, foster families, and chosen families. Paradoxically, we may get along better if we are aware of the differences in perceptions of who and what family means for us. In the end, we may be more resilient than we think if we have had some kind of family to lean on in the hard time of loss.

Many of us have now had numerous losses. This is where I've struggled. No matter how supportive my family was and how hard I've worked, I've faced some problems that had no solution: my little brother's death from polio; my sister's cancer; a loved one lost to addiction; a divorce; the loss of my parents, aunts and uncles, son-in-law, brother-in-law, and many lifelong friends. I have finally learned that things won't always go my way. I will lose people I love. What more have I learned? That not always having my way actually motivates me to become more inventive. I became more resilient.

And now, there is the death of my dear husband, not from COVID-19, but from a stroke. I am knocked down. And I will get up again.

CHAPTER 5

THE PARADOX OF ABSENCE AND PRESENCE

It's not right, a wife should wait ten years to find she's not.
—Jez Butterworth, *The Ferryman*

Having a loved one disappear is a devastating kind of loss because it's ambiguous. There is no certainty that the lost person is dead or alive, if they will return, or where they, or their remains, might be.

The ambiguity surrounding this kind of loss leads to high anxiety and feelings of helplessness and confusion. As a result, people might cope in extreme ways; mentally closing out the lost person as if they do not exist, or by denying the loss or its ambiguity. Yet, instead of these absolute reactions, many people learn to tolerate the ambiguity and live well despite it.

While this complicated type of loss can immobilize us and our families by freezing grieving and coping processes, there is a way to shift our thinking that helps us to live more calmly with uncertainty. This, however, requires us to grapple with the paradox of absence and presence.

With ambiguous loss, contradictions abound. The wife in the quote above has now waited 10 years to find out if her husband is dead or alive. He disappeared during the Troubles in Northern Ireland during the 1960s, so she was considered by others to be both a wife and not-a-wife. When her missing husband was finally found buried in a bog, she still had many unanswered questions, and the conflict continued. Her story of loss was without an ending.

Paradoxically, for families of the ambiguously lost, their yearning for closure with an absolute answer often increases their suffering as it stirs up conflict with one another, or even with authorities. In the absence of facts, differing theories flourish and lead to conflict. In families, this creates alienation. On a national scale, this can create rebellion.

The good news is that while the sadness of loss never goes away entirely, we do better if we understand the contradictions of paradox. It helps to know that instead of neat and precise endings, the reality of loss comes in complicated shades of gray. A family member or friend can be both present and absent at the same time. Someone who is sitting near us can be gone cognitively and emotionally if they have advanced dementia or are addicted to drugs or alcohol. Or loved ones who are physically absent can still be present in our hearts and minds. Said another way, the present can be absent, and the absent can be present. This is the paradox of human relationships.

Today, the pandemic has done just that. While we were

more divided than since the Civil War, with conflict in families and a mob storming our nation's capital, we learned about absurdity and paradox. Presence and absence, facts and fiction, were muddled. Even a leader was ambiguously lost, missing in action. Who was in charge and who was not was unclear for far too long.

During the time of pandemic, families and friends used video calls to be present with others who were somewhere else; parents loved the time at home with the kids while also yearning to be alone; they went to work while remaining at home and helping the kids with their lessons. People were both absent and present to each other. In all of this time, the most painful absurdity was that many people had to say goodbye to a loved one who was ill, sometimes for the last time, through a glass window or cell phone.

Worse yet, at a time when millions needed to grieve the loss of family members, friends, mentors, or coworkers, our usual rituals of comfort were forbidden. During the pandemic, when deaths spiked and then spiked again and again, and when mourners needed it most, a funeral became dangerous to their health—the ultimate paradox. In times of crisis, contradictions become the norm.

To make sense of this time in history, it helps to face the absurdity and contradictions of not only what sickened and killed, but of all that was going on then and now. There was and still is much vagueness swirling around, even bald misinformation and conspiracy theories, about the virus. People lost their health to COVID-19, but still refused to wear a mask; scientists and medical workers were often demonized;

some said the pandemic was a hoax when facts were staring them in the face. Absurdity reigned. Paradoxically, the sickness was not understanding the sickness.

The cause of our anxiety now is not our weakness but rather the tumultuous environment around us, with multiple crises—medical, social, economic, and racial—all happening at the same time, all life threatening and seriously urgent. Such a context understandably heightens human anxiety, depression, and anger.

To withstand such troubled times, we need resilience. We have to stay strong and flexible to withstand the virus, but now, even when it is being controlled with the vaccines, we have to stay resilient to face and deal with our other societal problems: systemic racism; increasing poverty in a rich country; and widespread disparities in who has health insurance and access to proper medical care, housing, education, and broadband internet. Ironically, during this pandemic, the rich were getting richer while even the middle classes joined the food lines. Our need for the resilience and flexibility to change our ways does not end with the pandemic.

Change is inherently stressful because it requires us to be open and flexible to new ways and ideas. Transformation often requires compromise, so it tests our tolerance for the less than perfect. Not always getting exactly what we want is a test of ambiguity tolerance.

It's easy to deny what we can't see, what is invisible, or what is not in our range of knowing, but to change, we may have to face the stress of ambiguity squarely. We gather as much information as we can about our losses, past and present, so we know what the problems are and what we're dealing with. Sometimes, however, there is no clarifying information about a loss, so we may have to discover new ways to find it.

After 9/11, when the Twin Towers in New York City were attacked and then collapsed, a grandmother told me of her little grandson and how distraught he was when his father did not come home on that terrible day. He didn't cry but was frantic to go and find his daddy and bring him back home. He believed that if he were allowed to look for him, he could find him. He was angry because no one was taking him down to Ground Zero to allow him to search for his father. Finally, his wise grandmother found a way to take him to Ground Zero to see the fallen towers where his father had worked. On the way down on a ferry, obviously hopeful of finding his father, the little boy was excited, but as they approached lower Manhattan, he grew quiet and then, for the first time, began sobbing. Seeing the mountains of smoking rubble, he realized for the first time that he would never be able to find his missing father.

To be sure, facing such horrendous loss is painful, but paradoxically, that raw pain, awful as it is, leads to less pain over time. We don't get over such loss, but we learn to live with it. I wonder where that boy is today, and if, as a man now, he has found some measure of peace about the loss of his father. I hope so.

To live with the paradox of absence and presence in your own relationships, it helps to think about and then list who and what you have lost—not just those losses that occurred during the pandemic, but also current losses and those from the past, especially from the first time that you can remember a loss that really hurt. Or from hearing your elders tell stories about their traumatic losses or those passed down across the generations. Write these losses down; reflect on them. They are part of your legacy. Hopefully, there are stories of resilience, but some may be of downfall or failure. All this begins your search for meaning. Acknowledging your feelings about these ancestral losses will help you deal with your current losses. Expect a range of feelings—confusion, sadness, grief, anger, guilt, pride, empathy, or simply peace.

If losses are not dealt with, the trauma of unresolved grief can be passed down from generation to generation. We see this transmission today of traumatizing losses incurred centuries ago—the genocide of Native Americans, the injustices and pain of slavery, the horrors of the Holocaust, plus endless wars, and genocides never officially acknowledged and thus still not resolved.

Likely, we and our children and grandchildren will never forget the losses caused by the 2020 pandemic; we will pass stories of both pain and healing on to future generations— just as my father did about the flu he had as a boy in the 1918 pandemic, and as I do still, about the polio epidemic that killed my little brother in the summer of 1955. There is purpose in the telling. We pass on our narratives about the paradox of absence and presence, of loss and resilience, because we don't want closure.

■ ■ ■

Throughout ancient literature, the paradox of how the missing can still be present is the stuff of many tales. Here's an example. Based on the *Aeneid*, as told by Uncle Pat in the Irish play *The Ferryman*, the people who are not dead but have gone missing are marooned on the shores of the river Styx waiting frantically to be rowed across. But the Ferryman can't carry them across the river because their status as dead or alive is ambiguous. As a result, they are abandoned on the shore and must roam the earth until there is certainty about their death.

The story about the Ferryman rowing the dead across the river Styx is an ancient one, but as I sat in a Broadway theater, watching this play, I wondered if this fear of missing loved ones not being able to rest in peace is the reason why some families, for generations, keep on searching for their missing soldiers. I was mesmerized by the veracity of this play, about the agony of such loss, in this case, during the Irish Troubles when young men routinely disappeared. When the play opened originally in London, I was asked to write an essay for the London playbill. This is an excerpt:

> *The paradox of how the missing can still be present is the stuff of countless tales throughout literature: as long ago as Sophocles' Antigone and now in Jez Butterworth's The Ferryman, characters are asked to confront the unimaginable. For Antigone, the question is how she can mourn her brother's death before being able to give his body a proper burial. For the Carney family in this play, the question is similar: how can the family members reach closure when there is no body to grieve?*

The answer is that they can't reach closure even after the body is found. That's not possible in real life either. Yet, stories about ambiguity and loss continue to hold our interest because they represent this all-too-common human experience. Playwrights, poets, and artists are inspired by the paradox of absence and presence, and audiences are mesmerized by it. We see it in theaters and art galleries and hear it in music. But in real life, contradictions hurt, and we fight for certainty. Perhaps this is why mystery stories are so popular; they always end with a clear and perfect solution.

Aside from plays and entertainment, we are, in the end, wrestling with ourselves to settle the paradox of absence and presence. Where is the person I care about? Who am I now that they have left me? Who am I now that I am divorced, unemployed, broke? Who am I now that my loved one has a terminal illness? How many children do I tell people I have if one was stillborn or disappeared, or refuses to see me? Who am I and what can I do now that the pandemic has changed my former way of life? For me, at 87, and newly widowed, I thought I had settled all this. But now, I need to find meaning again.

If we can find a measure of meaning in our losses and failures, we will feel more liberated to move forward in a new way. Of course, sorrow returns at times, especially at holidays, weddings, births, graduations—and even years later, when it causes us to shed a tear at something or some place that reminds us of the person or object we lost. But for all of us, choosing to accept the paradox of absence and presence is less painful than trying to find closure.

■ ■ ■

In our darkest moments, we often make the best progress in our own growth and resilience. As the ancient Chinese proverb says, "In every crisis there is opportunity." Even after the recent death of my dear husband in high old age, I live with ambiguous loss. He is gone but still here. I treasure that paradox. What this means is that I live with the sadness of his loss while I am also moving forward with my work, with thinking about what to do in the future I have left. I am reminded every day of his absence as the *New York Times* arrives or when I hear some music he liked. I still want to circle things in the morning paper that we would discuss later in the day, when his aides left and we were alone. Those were precious times.

At every turn, I am reminded of that life together, but while I am sad, I am not devastated. I do not have the trauma of ambiguity surrounding his death. I was there with him when he died; I have the proof of an official death certificate. His ashes are here for now. Not everyone has that benefit.

The contradictions of paradox can also be eased, if not resolved, by the fact that we can discover new ways of being. No matter our age, we can change. We can evolve and become even more resilient than we were before the deadly pandemic. Yes, change brings sadness, discomfort, disruption, and often anger, all of which we now see in the daily news and often in ourselves. But continuity and change, the ultimate contributors to paradox, must be recalibrated now and then and changed into something new. This shift is essential for the survival of any human system—individual, family, community, or country.

The more you face the absurdity of paradox in your losses— the need for both continuity and change—the more likely you will find meaning and purpose to move forward again with your life in an even better way than before the pandemic. What helps? A new way of thinking, the topic of Chapter 6.

CHAPTER 6

BOTH/AND THINKING

The test of a first-rate intelligence is the ability
to hold two opposed ideas in mind at the same
time, and still retain the ability to function.
  —F. Scott Fitzgerald, *The Crack-Up*

I n my clinical work, I routinely worked with families who were in conflict. I remember this one vividly. An elderly man, the head of a three-generation family, suffered from advanced dementia. His adult son said he could cope with his father as long as he considered him a piece of furniture and did not bump into him. I will never forget that response or what followed. The little grandson spoke up immediately, telling his father that he was wrong, that his grandfather was still here. That little boy was my cotherapist that day. He knew about both/and thinking while his father did not.

Both/and thinking means being able to hold two contra-dictory ideas in one's mind at the same time—just as Fitzgerald wrote. This grandfather's memory was gone, but he was still physically present—and alive. Here and yet gone. With such ambiguous loss, there is more than one possibility of truth, at least at that moment in time. It's not the binary of either total presence or total absence. It's both. People can be absent and present at the same time.

This way of thinking, however, can affect different people in different ways even in the same community, depending on social status and income. Sometimes we do not have the privilege of entertaining two options. With soldiers missing in action in the 1970s and the missing after 9/11, many families accepted death certificates for pragmatic and financial reasons. Yet, when I talked with them, their doubt was apparent. Most continued to say, "They're probably dead" and "maybe not."

When we think about the loss of a family member or friend as both/and, we may be reminded of dialectical thinking, which means holding both a thesis and antithesis but eventually reaching a synthesis or blending of those two opposing facts. With ambiguous loss, however, such opposing ideas may never blend and synthesize. This lack of having one precise answer is especially challenging for those who seek perfection.

Many of us have been trained to do just that: find the exact solution. While we may prefer such success, there are times, now and then, when there is no perfect solution. Some losses remain unclear forever, so we live with doubt.

It is important to know, therefore, that both/and thinking is not precisely the same as dialectical thinking. This is because synthesis may not be possible. Dialectical thinking assumes an eventual merging of the two opposing ideas, but this cannot happen with losses that remain ambiguous. We may wish for synthesis, but it may never happen. Rather than waiting for some resolution, then, we use the ongoing tension of conflicting ideas to provide the momentum to move us forward toward adaptation and change—living life in a new way without the lost person.

While absolute thinking divides people, both/and thinking can show us what we have in common. In this commonality lies the possibility of shifting to a middle ground. Some stress remains, but balancing two conflicting ideas in your mind at the same time is less stressful than continuing to search for one perfect solution.

When there is no one perfect answer or solution, it's useful to let go of the binary and move to that middle ground. For example, let go of such absolute thinking as, "He's dead to me; he's like a piece of furniture," and think instead, "He's both here and gone; both absent and present." In this way, we balance the negative with the positive and thus avoid being immobilized by anger or grief.

This way of thinking is more fluid, less absolute, and thus closer to the truth of ambiguous loss. It helps us find meaning enough to live with losses that have no apparent or immediate solution—like with the pandemic. But, even after this pandemic, there will continue to be physical and psychological losses as well as unanswered questions about death. This is not just from such extremes as war and plague, but simply from the stress of everyday life.

Without witnessing a loved one's death, or seeing them before they are buried or cremated or having DNA verification, people may keep hoping that the lost person might still be alive somewhere, that they might return. I saw this often with families of the missing after 9/11 in New York City and in Kosovo after the cruel kidnappings in the 1990s, as well as in Japan after the tsunami of 2011 washed away thousands of loved ones. We saw this kind of ambiguous loss again during the pandemic as loved ones were dying alone, bodies withheld or buried in unmarked graves. Worldwide, with so many victims of COVID-19 now buried in potter's fields, the ambiguous losses of this pandemic have skyrocketed.

A note of caution, however. The both/and way of thinking is not appropriate for every situation of loss. In competitive games and financial matters, for example, there is no ambiguity. It's either win or lose; gain or loss; success or failure. It was success or failure when we put a man on the moon and rovers on Mars. But in human relationships, and the loss of someone we love, such binaries won't help us find peace. We are more likely to find it in the middle ground, that gray area in between each extreme. Right now, I have certainty about my husband's death from the official certificate that just arrived in the mail, but I find comfort in that middle ground, too.

During this pandemic, the stress of ambiguity was evident everywhere—from the pressure to change one's routines and ways of working to the denial of COVID-19. Perhaps the most stressful was the politicization of those who refused to wear masks versus those who did and still do. As absurdity and rationality were at odds, our stress levels rose to crisis levels and immobilized us.

Regardless of what our disagreements were about how we saw loss during the pandemic, it still benefits us to manage our frustration and stress. We do this by continuing to use both/and thinking: I am both leaving home to go to work and spending time with my kids; I am both hungry for alone time and for social contacts; I both disagree with my neighbor and continue talking with him. I am both stressed with a world weariness and also optimistic that things are slowly getting better.

When faced with problems right now that have no solution, we have to manage the stress they cause. Loss of our freedom to do as we please requires change, and change is stressful, especially when it wasn't our idea. The core idea is that we can cope if we know what the problem is, have enough resilience to withstand the stress, and can balance our individual needs with a concern for others.

Medical sociologist and stress expert Aaron Antonovsky said that if we think something is understandable, manageable, and meaningful, the stress it causes is less debilitating to one's health. This means there is good stress and bad stress. Some people choose to experience high stress; they enjoy competitive sports, even extreme sports, and taking risks. They would call this good stress because they can manage it.

At a University of Zurich conference in 1993, however, we were discussing bad stress, stress that is not wanted. Antonovsky agreed that ambiguous loss was highly stressful and harmful, and told us why: it was because of its lack of manageability and coherence or logic. We both presented our ideas at the conference, and afterward continued talking about the incoherence of ambiguous loss over coffee at a nearby restaurant. We were so deep in discussion, as professors are known to do, that we left the restaurant without noticing the check. The waiter came flying outside, his long white apron flapping as he ran after us, waving the check and yelling in Swiss German that we had not paid our bill— and we must! Like obedient children, we quickly and apologetically settled the bill. Then, after saying goodbye, we went our separate ways. That was the last time I saw Professor Antonovsky, as he died the next year. Yet, as I write this chapter, I keep thinking about that discussion. He reaffirmed the idea of the necessity of being able to make sense of and manage one's stress, and why ambiguity prevents that. And why ambiguity then can be so incapacitating to one's health: It's impossible to make sense of it.

■ ■ ■

When all the world's people have been overcome by something more powerful than themselves—a deadly virus—and when everyone who is accustomed to being in charge of their own lives suddenly has to submit to rules, like mandated lockdowns and wearing masks, we see more aggressive behavior and more denial that anything is wrong. Conspiracy theories flourish. Scapegoats are blamed, an indicator of needing an absolute answer for the cause of one's trouble. Instead, we should externalize the blame. The culprit during this pandemic has been a new and mutating virus and the ambiguity it is still causing; no need to blame each other.

What we all have in common at such times is that none of us wants to be dominated by an outside force. But the virus became just that—a dominating force that is still a danger to many in the world who are not yet vaccinated. How do we handle this?

When faced with a problem that can't be changed, at least right away, we can change our way of thinking because that's all we can change. Instead of absolute thinking, we shift to both/and thinking. This is resilience—being open to change; being able to hold two opposing ideas in your mind at the same time, as F. Scott Fitzgerald wrote. Doing this is immensely useful when some outside force is wearing us down.

Consider the case of family caregivers. Today, millions of women, men, and teenagers are taking care of family members who have a terminal illness, a physical or psychological ailment, or some disability. Such illnesses or conditions become the dominant stressor for that family and alter every aspect of their routines and way of life. Whether it's taking care of an elderly parent, a terminally ill partner, or a child with a serious illness, it's another version of what we all felt with COVID-19—our lives are dominated by an outside force. When illness controls our lives, or the lives of those we care for, we can't always have our way. Parents of newborns and caregivers of frail elders all know the feeling. Whether we choose these responsibilities or not, caregivers no longer have the freedom to do as they please. (Who are these people anyway who think they can always do as they please? They are not the people who care for young children or the sick and dying.)

To maintain their own health, caregivers learn early about the need for both/and thinking. In groups, they learn to externalize the blame to the illness or condition that caused the need for care, and then find the middle ground. "I will both care for my loved one and take care of myself." This is not an easy task. In my own experience of caregiving for several years, I learned it was easier to write a book about caregiving than to do it. My empathy for family caregivers definitely grew.

A distraught man in a caregiving group once told me he was at his wits' end taking care of his wife for over a year. She had Alzheimer's disease. He was retired but had given up his Thursday afternoon golfing with his friends to do caregiving. I asked why he didn't continue his Thursday afternoon off. Was it cost? No, he said. It was his guilt. He thought it was selfish to want some time off with his friends. What would people say? My recommendation: Take Thursdays off; golf with your friends. You can both be a good caregiving husband and take care of yourself. Paradoxically, taking time off is a gift to your ill wife; she will have a happier and healthier caregiver and husband.

Dominated by the illness of a loved one, caregivers often give up anything that is for their own benefit, that keeps them connected to others and healthy. While they often feel isolated and controlled, they also feel guilty about caring for their own needs. This is perhaps the greatest danger for caregivers. They take care of their loved one but not of themselves. That would require holding those two opposing ideas in one's mind at the same time, not an easy task. They succumb to the domination of the illness or disability for which they provide care, being overcome by something more powerful than themselves. In a sense, being a caregiver is similar to other situations when we're not in control of our own lives—all require the flexibility of both/and thinking to survive.

Surprisingly, people both young and old pick up this way of thinking quite readily. They know the in-between is closer to reality than either extreme. During the pandemic, so much was irrational, so we needed to know that the situation was pathological, not those experiencing it. The pandemic was both restricting and growth producing. It both restricted us from doing our usual activities of life and freed us to do something new and different. An actress taught a new improv class on Zoom, this time for cancer patients; a waitress who lost her job finished her bachelor's degree; many people learned to bake sourdough bread; a furloughed pilot cooked dinners for his family. He said it was both a negative and positive experience; he was both restricted from flying and having more quality time with his kids.

As we try to make sense of the time of pandemic, thinking both/and will continue to help us. It was both a terrible time and a time of growth; it was both a time of loss and a time of gaining new insight. It was both a time of current loss and a time of reckoning for past and present losses for people of color. For me, it was both a time of painful personal loss, the death of my husband, and a time of new learning about larger-scale losses.

Even when this pandemic is over, we will not have closure. Loss has left its mark on us and changed the ways we think and live. The novel coronavirus has both taken from us and given us something new. For me, that is the humility of knowing once again that I am not always in control.

CHAPTER 7

SIX GUIDELINES FOR THE RESILIENCE TO LIVE WITH LOSS

When we are no longer able to change a situation . . .
we are challenged to change ourselves.

—Viktor Frankl, *Man's Search for Meaning*

When losses remain ambiguous, as so many do, the only window for change lies in our perception, how we see a loss. Once we realize we have the power to shift our view, we're able to adjust it to one that is less laden with guilt, anger, or the need for revenge. Paradoxically, we change because our loss will not.

This process takes time, but movement is essential. The journey is circular, not linear, and can be random in order. But the end goal is increasing our resilience. This is the ability to withstand the pain of loss and the anxiety of ambiguity, get up again after we've been knocked down, and grow stron-

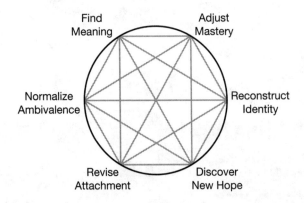

Figure 7.1.
Guidelines for Increasing Resilience to Live with Loss

ger from the suffering. The process of building resilience can apply to any human group, from individuals to families to a nation to the whole world.

To see the possibilities in how to live with loss, we embrace paradox and use both/and thinking, and then follow six psychosocial guidelines based on meaning, mastery, identity, ambivalence, attachment, and new hope. Each guideline is meant to be used as needed, with no prescribed order, but eventually, try to attend to all six (Figure 7.1).

In no particular order, as indicated by the various connecting lines in Figure 7.1, the following guidelines can help build your resilience: finding meaning, adjusting need for mastery, reconstructing identity, normalizing ambivalence, revising attachment, and discovering new hope. Meaning and hope are linked, thus the circular diagram. Perhaps because finding meaning is one of the most difficult to achieve, I recommend beginning by asking yourself this question: "What does this loss mean to me?" Your answer may change over time. But make this circle journey your own. Begin where you need to begin. Go back and forth as you need. The six guidelines are *not* stages, rules, or linear, but simply meant to guide you on your journey to find meaning and new hope in loss and grief.

Find Meaning

Finding meaning in loss takes time as it's a process of trying to make sense out of the loss. This is most challenging, if not impossible, with ambiguous loss, but it's also a challenge with ordinary loss. While unanswered questions are formidable with ambiguous loss, some exist even with ordinary loss, for example, the death of a grandparent. Why wasn't I there? Did I do enough? Did I say what I needed to say? What did they mean when they said their last words? Were they proud of me? The key question, however, is always this: What does this loss mean to me? Do I see it as fate, destiny, an act of God, the benevolent ending of a painful illness, or simply the end of a long life well lived? Was it a relief? A surprise? A blessing? A punishment? Meaning differs based on your context.

By context, I mean that a loss will mean different things depending on where and how it happens and what caused it. Was the person killed in the line of duty, or killed in sacrifice and heroism, or killed by a drunk driver or unjustly by police? Perhaps most difficult to understand are losses that are out of order, or outside of the realm of human expectations—

infant death, friendly fire, murder, suicide, genocide. In these kinds of losses, meaning is especially hard to find.

Some losses, therefore, never make sense, so naming them "meaningless" becomes their meaning. Labeling them as such tells us the problem lies in the context—one of irrationality, ambiguity, absurdity, senselessness. In such cases, feelings of helplessness are common. Our best option, then, is to cope through some kind of *action*—seeking justice, working for a cause, or demonstrating to right the wrong.

For my family, in 1955, our cause was the March of Dimes. After my little brother died of polio, we all went door to door collecting dimes to fund research for a vaccine. Today, the focus is on other diseases, but still many people continue to join causes to help raise research funds to cure or eradicate the disease that caused their love one's suffering or death. Sometimes this is the only way to find meaning in what is otherwise a meaningless loss. Such movements, along with the many today that seek cures for illnesses such as pancreatic cancer, Alzheimer's and Parkinson's disease, and a host of others, can help people find meaning in what would otherwise be meaningless loss.

In addition, public acknowledgment of one's loss through memorials, large and small, elegant and humble, also help to bring meaning to senseless loss. The National Memorial for Peace and Justice, often called the National Lynching Memorial, and the Legacy Museum in Montgomery, Alabama; the Holocaust museums around the world; the Oklahoma City National Memorial of chairs of those lost to the domestic terrorist bombing in 1995; and the 9/11 Memorial and Museum in New York City, with names of the dead and missing and a waterfall flowing down into a void, all help us find a measure of meaning for losses that will never make sense. After this pandemic, we will need memorials, too, to acknowledge and honor the dead.

Overall, to find meaning for both the dead and the still missing, we must know what it is we are grieving. That the person we love is gone, or that we don't know for sure since there is no evidence of certainty. But even if you have doubts, finding meaning is still possible, especially if you use both/ and thinking. This is fortunate because meaning is central for human motivation and well-being.

What psychologists tell us is that for most people, life is "pretty meaningful," even for those who have faced hard times. Said another way, we find meaning even through suffering. Viktor Frankl found meaning in a concentration camp; Antonovksy found it in hospitals working with cancer patients. Many find meaning in action, doing something to prevent others from suffering as they did. Whether for ourselves or for others, finding meaning and purpose in tragedy makes that tragedy easier to bear. That's resilience. The pain of loss can make us stronger.

How do we make sense of our losses? In the early days of the pandemic, we had difficulty finding meaning because information was blocked. Truth became an ambiguous loss. We yearned to hear from scientists. Meaning and purpose, however, were found in helping each other to stay healthy. We used our ingenuity to find some joy in each day even though many of us were alone. This was a horrible time, but for those of us who have survived, we can now find meaning by grieving and remembering those who did not.

We grieve individually and we grieve as a nation because, as President Biden said on the eve of his inauguration in a ceremony honoring those who died in the pandemic, "It's hard sometimes to remember. But that's how we heal. It's important to do that as a nation." While we grieve, there is also the meaning for most of us that systemic changes are needed to make life better for all. Likely, we all agree that we'll never forget this time.

The meaning of living through a pandemic, for me, is that we are not always in charge, that we can't always have our way, and that we actually can endure suffering, not only to survive, but to discover that we have even gained more empathy for the plight of others. Perhaps you found this meaning, too.

Adjust Mastery

I think of the Serenity Prayer: "God, give us grace to accept with serenity the things that cannot be changed, courage to change things that should be changed, and the wisdom to distinguish the one from the other."

Mastery is the ability to master challenges and have control over our lives. This, however, is a privilege not everyone has. Poverty, famine, war, discrimination, or disasters, for example, can take away one's actual mastery and control. In order to know how to cope, it is useful to understand your own need for power and control now.

First, consider the extremes of mastery. On the high side, there is the need for perfectionism or domination; on the low side, there is passivity or submission. Neither of these extremes is useful after loss, but we all need enough mastery to manage the situation at hand. Being able to manage and solve problems is consistently shown to ease stress and trauma.

What we know now is that the higher our need for mastery, the more devastated we can be by uncontrollable events that happen to us. Author Joan Didion wrote of her lifelong fear of not being able to control or manage some events. Yet she was realistic and knew something like an uncontrollable event would just happen one day. When her husband died suddenly at the dinner table, she wrote, "This was one of those events. You sit down to dinner and life as you know it ends."

Early on in the pandemic, we saw that life as we knew it was indeed uncontrollable and had drastically changed. I had to rethink my own needs for mastery and control. (I thought of my Calvinistic mother who taught me that if I worked hard enough, I could solve anything. Not so.) When faced with the power of a deadly virus, our sense of mastery had to be tempered. Unable to control the virus as it first spread, most of us adapted and lowered our personal need for control, put on a mask, avoided large crowds, and stayed home for more than a year. We did this because it helped master our safety against the virus, and the safety of others. Many others did not see it that way and rebelled, seeing masks as infringing on their own sense of personal freedom. This may have increased the death toll. While many saw mastery as doing their own thing, many others saw mastery as taking precautions to protect themselves and others.

Even in normal times, however, there are differences in views about staying in charge of one's life. People who work hard and still can't succeed are often judged as lazy or causing their own failure. Yet their lack of mastery over the situation is often due to discrimination based on race, gender, sexual orientation, disability, or age. Some people have less mastery over their lives, not because they want less, but because they are without resources or opportunities. They are not permitted to be empowered often due to prejudice and poverty. For example, women and girls in some cultures are not allowed to be educated and thus are less able to keep themselves safe from abuse and harm. They need more mastery, not less.

What I find is that the more we try to control the pain of loss, clear or ambiguous, the more it dominates us. It is better to flow with the sorrow when it comes, have a good cry, and afterward, carry on again as best you can. No pressure. Emotional ups and downs are natural. If we allow them to be felt, the downs become farther and farther apart over time, easing but never totally done.

Some time ago, I heard from a friend whose son went missing in the mountains of Idaho, and later was found dead. He told me that his grief counselors were encouraging him to be more vulnerable, and then added, "Of course, that's an unnatural act for me." I smiled and understood immediately; this grieving father was a retired U.S. Navy captain trained to solve every problem. I told him that as a military officer, he was expected to master and control the most difficult situations, but the loss of his son was different. It was not something he could have controlled or could control now. It was not his failure. Trying to master his grief would not work. Grief is meant to be expressed and lived with, not controlled.

Americans are known for their optimism and ingenuity, so we take pride in our ability to master the big challenges. Space engineers have taken a sample of rocks from the asteroid Bennu—so far away that it will take three years for the rocks to get back to earth for testing. Mastering and controlling disease is not as clear. Thus far, only one disease—smallpox—has been eradicated worldwide. Polio is nearly eliminated but still occurs where vaccines are mistrusted. With the COVID-19 virus, if more people take a vaccine, it may no longer be a deadly pandemic but may become endemic, causing only mild illnesses, like colds or seasonal flu. No closure it seems even on the COVID-19 virus. We do not have the power to destroy the virus, but we do have the power to lessen *its* impact on us. Unfortunately, some still view accepting vaccinations as a threat to their freedom, so they refuse. Mastery has now been passed down from the scientists and medical experts to citizens who must decide for themselves—and the good of their neighbors—whether or not to accept immunity.

Medical professionals and health care workers are trained to cure human illness and disease, so it is understandable that when a patient dies, they often view it as their failure. During the pandemic, medical professionals and health care workers toiled long hours under horrific conditions to save the lives of pandemic patients. Their care and treatments were masterful even though they worked in dangerously crowded hospitals. They did not always succeed but did their best and learned by trial and error what worked and what did not. That too is mastery, mastery by innovation, under terrible pressure. Indeed, the heroes of this pandemic are the doctors and nurses who discovered new treatments and the scientists who created vaccines.

Reconstruct Identity

Knowing who we are in relation to a lost loved one requires reconstructions in mind and emotions about who we are, what we do, and how we act. Who am I now that my loved one has died? Am I still the child if I am caring for my parent? Am I still married if my spouse has gone missing? Or has died? What are my family roles, rituals, and rules now?

When my husband died, these questions became real for me. A decade ago, when he needed care, I shifted my identity as solely his wife to also being his caregiver. Now that he has died, I need to shift again. My identity now is neither wife nor caregiver, but widow. This new way of being feels strange to me, like putting on a heavy coat that doesn't quite fit. It will take some time to build a new identity. I will get there.

People diagnosed with terminal illnesses who then went into remission also say it takes time. They tell me they had to shift their identity when they thought they were dying, and again after their treatment worked and their disease went into remission. Such changes in seeing ourselves and who we can be, occur because of ambiguous gain as well as ambiguous loss. Like the terminally ill patient in remission, COVID-19 patients may have similar shifts in identity after nearly dying. If they identified with those who said the virus was a hoax, they may now have changed their minds about how they see themselves.

As life presents new challenges now that vaccines are here, the critical question is this: Am I resilient enough to change who I am, what I think, who my community is, and who I identify with? Can I be kind to someone who does not believe as I believe? Children grow up. Parents die. Our mates die. Over a lifetime, loss and change accumulate, so we must be malleable enough to grow and shift who we are and what we do. We do this to survive, but more is involved than just ourselves.

Identity is socially constructed. Who we are is shaped by the people around us. Thus, isolation will not help. To cope with loss and change in who we are and what we do, telling your story and listening to others will help. Try out new identities, listen to others who give you feedback—a therapist, counselor, or peers. Others serve as a mirror as you discover who you are now.

For example, family identities and roles have shifted greatly due to social pressures from the feminist movement that no longer link family roles—cooking, childcare, earning income—to gender. Unlike the women of my day who typically called themselves homemakers, that moniker is now less common. Family identities are more often now based on sharing tasks, a practical flexibility that leads to more resilient couples and families.

What to do? Discover how much flexibility you have to

change or not change. In my case, a legal document won't allow me to check the "married" box anymore. I would have to bend and check the "widow" box. So that's clear. No flexibility there. What is your situtation? Who has empathy and support for you? Your kinfolk, friends, colleagues at work or far away, a clergyperson, a therapist or counselor? Find someone to act as your mirror, giving feedback on who you are trying to become after loss. Tell your story to someone you trust and listen to their response.

For now, I struggle with reconstructing my identity because I loved what I had. I am forever an academic, a family therapist, mother and grandmother, a stepmother, a sister, an aunt, a great aunt, a cousin. But as I just found out, I am no longer a wife. That identity is gone.

It's too soon for me to say how I will change who I am and what I do, but I have been abruptly reminded once again how painful it is to reconstruct one's identity. Over my lifetime, I have gone from single to married to divorced to married again and now widowed. No longer am I the wife of the man I married, nor am I his caregiver. I am now a widow who must find a new way of being. A difficult shift at my age, but it will come.

Normalize Ambivalence

In psychology, ambivalence means having conflicting feelings and emotions at the same time. We simultaneously feel love/hate, pleasure/pain, or both anger and love toward the same person. The poet Sharon Olds wrote about her dying father: "I wanted to watch my father die because I hated him. Oh, I loved him." Linda Gray Sexton, daughter of poet Anne Sexton, wrote of her ambivalence when she saw her usually depressed mother on stage and fully present for her audience. "In that moment I hated her and her power absolutely. In that moment I loved her and her power absolutely."

Ambivalence is the child of ambiguity. In the absence of clarity about a loss, there are mixed emotions about the lost person such as anger/sorrow or love/hate. Such conflicting emotions can cause immobilizing guilt and anxiety, so it is necessary to talk with someone to acknowledge and manage that negative side of ambivalence.

While psychological ambivalence is not considered a disorder, it can lead to hesitancy, confusion, indecision, and procrastination, each of which can be problematic. For example, if we have a high tolerance for ambiguity, we may not be immobilized by conflicting thoughts. But if we are binary thinkers and like precise answers, we may exhibit so much distress from ambivalent feelings that we rush to absolute solutions, like denying that anything is wrong or needing closure on the matter.

Whenever I worked with people experiencing ambiguous loss, I also saw ambivalence and normalized it. Most often, it was caused not by personal deficiency, but by the contradictions that emerged from an environment of confusion around them. This is "social ambivalence." Context matters. Ambivalence does not result just from worrying about making a wrong decision, but often from a social environment that blocks our ability to make that decision. This social-psychological view of ambivalence externalizes the cause and creates less resistance in acknowledging our mixed emotions.

If we live in contexts of confusion and ambiguity, it helps to acknowledge our mixed emotions so that we can more likely manage our anxiety and guilt. It takes mental strength and resilience to manage such uncomfortable feelings. Social psychologist Leon Festinger called this discomfort "cognitive dissonance." Yet not all contradictory thoughts increase our stress. For families of the disappeared, when there is no alternative, holding conflicting ideas is often less stressful than the alternative—denying that anything is wrong or concluding prematurely that the person is dead and never returning. In such cases, being in a state of ambivalence may actually lower one's stress. But there is an important caveat: Holding on to our contradictory feelings about even a lost person requires us to change and move forward with life in a new way. We cannot just wait. We cannot continue to hope for what was.

Unfortunately, ambivalent feelings can divide people. Binary thinkers are less likely to compromise or hold conflicted feelings. In the continuing environment of anger and lies dividing our nation, it's no wonder that conflicted emotions are trickling down to our families and friends. Vehement disagreements erupt. You love them and, at the same time, hate them for their beliefs. When you see them, you feel happy and sad at the same time. What we should not do is shut the door on each other permanently. Keep the door open. Ghosting is not the solution.

To heal ourselves and our families from this unprecedented time of ambiguity, we need leaders at all levels—family, community, nation, world—who can acknowledge ambivalent feelings, see them as inevitable, and nevertheless move forward with change for the greater good. Ambivalence may even be useful as it allows for compromise, essential in a democracy and in families.

Whether we are actively involved in politics or at home caring for a child or a frail elder, it is normal to have some ambivalent feelings about how to act, what to do, what to believe. We must also be aware, however, that hesitation can lead to inaction, and thus decrease our personal agency to better our situation. This is why I have always coupled both/and thinking and paradox with moving forward. We cannot hesitate or wait for our situation of loss to become clear. We have to make the best decisions possible even though they may not be perfect.

Revise Attachment

Psychologist John Bowlby, founder of attachment theory, wrote this about widows and widowers and the value of continuing bonds: "It is precisely because they are willing for their feelings of attachment to the dead spouse to persist that their sense of identity is preserved and they become able to reorganize their lives along lines they find meaningful." Again, the paradox. Continuing bonds with loved ones who died allows us to move forward with life.

When people have been deeply attached to each other, and one dies, there is a reluctance to let go. I feel that now, a few months after my husband died. It doesn't feel like an ending but more like a transition. Even though he is clearly gone, the wedding ring I gave him is now on my middle finger next to the ring he gave to me. It is for me a symbol of that enduring bond. Professionally, I know about the paradox of loss, but now, personally, for me it's new again. I know that he is gone; I was with him when he took his last breath. But symbolically, he's still here with me.

Contrary to what some may think, finding joy in life after the loss of someone you love doesn't mean the end of that attachment. There is no need to seek closure, even if other relationships develop. We are, after all, an accumulation of all the relationships we have had over our lifetime. It's possible to hold them all—the old and the new, the good and the bad—in the same sphere, for they are all part of who we have become.

The task is to let go of the person we lost but keep them present in our heart and mind as we gradually rebuild our lives in new ways. But this takes time—and thus requires patience on the part of those around us. Hopefully, we will eventually find some new purpose in life, make new friends, or participate in a new project or cause. Or the goal may just be continuing to live with gratitude and joy because the person you lost cannot.

Today, we hear many stories of loved ones who couldn't safely see each other during the long pandemic. All too common was the agony of knowing a loved one was dying but not being allowed to be with them to say goodbye. With this, plus not being allowed to have the comfort of a funeral, trauma was added to a mourner's grief. And there was more. When we weren't allowed to be with the people we love for over a year, loneliness became as prevalent as the virus.

My husband was hospitalized for non-COVID-19 issues, but my time with him was also restricted. I could see him, but only for a short time, and only if I was in protective gear. Sadly, this made normal touching nearly impossible. I regret that still. In his last days, he was moved, and I was able to see him more often. I was grateful to be with him to the end and knew that many others in hospitals were not allowed that opportunity.

Again, culture plays a part in how we think about loved ones who have died. For revising attachment after death, Eastern cultures often encourage staying in touch with ancestors who perform symbolic roles, such as watching over family members, especially infants and children, who disappeared or died. More Western views tend toward closure, getting over loss, and being productive again. For many in our American culture, there is a discomfort with suffering. Whether a loss is ours or someone else's, we may see it as failure, and become impatient with the grief that follows.

Given the grim numbers of global pandemic deaths, we need patience and empathy now for the millions of families who are grieving. And if we are the bereaved, we need more patience with ourselves. Don't accept the idea of closure, but rather, slowly begin to revise your attachment to the person who died. Whether that attachment was secure or tenuous, accept the reality of loss. They are gone; life as it was has changed. Our connection to the lost person has changed. Left behind, we face the "savage pain."

Discover New Hope

If someone you love has been missing physically or psychologically for some time, try to begin hoping for something new, something that gives you the impetus to stop waiting and move ahead with your life in a new way. For this reason, I use the phrase "discover *new* hope." The goal is to discover something new to hope for. In working over four decades with people experiencing various kinds of ambiguous losses, I saw little resistance when asking them to imagine something new for their future. It seemed to motivate them, give them hope, not for recovering the lost person, but for recovering themselves. The questions I asked were: What is your life like now without this person? What could you be or do now? What have you always wanted to do but could not? Who were you before this relationship? I saw caregivers explore how their lives might be, if for the first time, they thought about their own needs. I saw partners of the missing after 9/11 who were now in charge of the family and needing to be breadwinners think about going back to school to learn a trade or profession. This kind of brainstorming is best done in the company of others experiencing the same kind of loss, or with a therapist, but it is not impossible to do it alone.

What I saw was astonishing creativity in this search for some new hope. For example, after 9/11, women whose husbands were missing babysat for one another so they could go to school to learn English or train for a job. They were now the breadwinners and such creative cooperation allowed new hopes to become reality.

While families of the missing discovered these new hopes and dreams, most still wanted to hold on to some doubt about the finality of their loss. "He is both gone, and still here with me." By not pathologizing such thinking, they said they felt respected. They could keep their doubts, not in an obsessive way, but because at that time it was as close to the truth as they could get.

Yet, both/and thinking alone will not lead to new hope. It will work only if it motivates you to take action and move ahead with new purpose and human connections. By itself, both/and thinking is not enough, but it can empower you to imagine living life in a new way without the lost person.

Until there is a body or DNA evidence, or medical evidence of remission from a terminal illness, no one knows for sure the fate of a person who remains ambiguously lost. If we respect and acknowledge the ambiguity in such losses, the people left behind won't feel so alone. With less isolation and more support, resilience grows. They are less likely to persist in waiting and more likely to see possibilities in changing. In other words, we can't just hang on to the outcome we want. That's harmful to ourselves and others who depend on us. Instead of obsessively hoping for life to return as it was, we have to hope for something new.

Finally, we need to be aware that profound loss can still occur even after a missing person is found. I think of the Tom Hanks film, *Cast Away*, and numerous real life cases—the few 9/11 missing found alive, and the many missing-in-action from all wars found either alive or dead—like Francine du Plessix Gray's pilot father who went missing during World War II. Years later, she found him buried in a grave in France. In *Cast Away*, a FedEx employee is stranded after his plane crashes on a deserted island in the South Pacific. Against all odds, he survives, and years later, is rescued. He returns home only to find his fiancée is now married to someone else. There is another painful loss for both of them. For the formerly missing man, his only option is imagining a new life.

Change happens even when hopes come true. When a missing person is found or when girls kidnapped by terrorists return home and are stigmatized by their families or village, the reversal of loss is also painful—and requires change. What we need to hope for is not to go back to what we had, but to see what we can create now and in the future. Don't wait. Spend time interacting with others to explore your options. Brainstorm with others. Try out new things. Imagine what life could be like if you are willing to risk change. Hope for something new and purposeful that will sustain you and give you joy for the rest of your life.

■ ■ ■

With the guidelines for resilience clarified, finding meaning has linked with discovering new hope. In between and in random order, as in Figure 7.1, are the ideas of mastery, identity, ambivalence, and attachment, all of which influence our ability to cope with loss and grief. All are meant to strengthen our resilience so we can bear the pain of loss.

I emphasize again that these guidelines are not meant to be used in a linear fashion, nor in any prescribed order. Nor are they stages because stages imply a finishing point—and there is none with grief. Pick the guideline that applies to you right now and start there. But know that meaning and new hope are linked. Paraphrasing Viktor Frankl, there is no meaning without hope and no hope without meaning. You can't have one without the other. May this circle of guidelines help to lighten your load as you carry the sorrow of loss and grow stronger for it.

CHAPTER 8

IF NOT CLOSURE,
WHAT'S NORMAL GRIEF?

Although mourning involves grave departures from the normal
attitude toward life, it never occurs to us to regard it as a
pathological condition and to refer it to a medical treatment.
      —Freud, "Mourning and Melancholia"

So far, I have not written much about grief, as this book is mostly about loss and its nuances. But it's time now. In 2020, headlines read: "Virus Crisis Explodes; 'Desperate' Situation." "Deaths Climb Fast . . . ; 'Horrifying' Toll." As of this writing, in summer 2021, refrigerator trailers are still being used in some regions and countries as morgues overflow. Worldwide, over 4 million people have died from COVID-19 and its mutations. Whether or not we are aware of it, we are in a world of grief. We are a nation in grief.

How can we grieve normally in abnormal times? I am trying to find out how to do this myself. Professionally, I was taught about the pathologies of grief but not much about what's normal. I know culture shapes how we grieve, so the answer to how we grieve normally differs for each of us.

■ ■ ■

I don't often drive back to my original hometown of New Glarus, Wisconsin, anymore. What I do there now is mostly tend graves—the graves of my Swiss American parents who both died in old age, the grave of my older sister who died too young, and the grave of my little brother, Eddie, who died at age 13.

Eddie's death also came during another plague, the polio epidemic of the 1950s. As much as I wanted the pain to go away, his death was my first lesson in the myth of closure. I knew I would never forget his smile, his energy, his likability, his endearing mischievousness. While Eddie died 66 years ago, I was reminded often of his loss during this pandemic. Eddie's last photo sits on the shelf above me now as I write, but mostly, I think of him when I am with my other brother, John. He and Eddie were buddies, born 11 months apart and inseparable. Because my mother had so much work to do, the boys were in my charge. In their early teens, they went to summer camp together, and shortly after that, Eddie got sick and died. It seemed just that fast. It was. Like many COVID-19 deaths.

I was by then a 19-year-old college student on the University of Wisconsin–Madison campus where Eddie was hospitalized. Unlike with COVID-19, I could visit him. He was encased in an iron lung in a huge room full of children, all inside similar tubelike machines. Eddie was surviving only because a machine was breathing for him. Only his head was outside the iron lung, so I stroked his hair and told him I loved him. He could not respond. He had bulbar polio, the worst kind, which affected his brain stem. And then after only a few days, he died. I was devastated. I remember saying out loud to myself, "I'll never be happy again."

After Eddie's funeral, it seemed the whole town crowded into our small house, including all the members of Eddie's junior high football team who had carried his coffin. I slipped outside to be alone. No one interrupted my crying, and fortunately, no one told me it was rude to withdraw, or that it was "God's will" or that "time would help me forget." And yet so much was said for me and my family by the simple presence of so many neighbors and friends—and what they so kindly did for us. Bringing food, driving us, doing the chores. Back then, in our Swiss American community, actions spoke louder than words. That is still true for some cultures today.

I tell you this story because I want you to know that while I was devastated by that loss, I have been indeed happy again—many times. I have had an extraordinarily good life despite many losses. I also tell you this story because you, too, may have experienced the death of a loved one or coworker or neighbor during the pandemic or any time before or after. I want to be frank: you can be knocked down and eventually get up again to have a good life, but you'll never be completely over the loss of someone you have loved. There is no closure, nor is there a need for it. Instead, we remember them and learn to live with the ambiguity of absence and presence. You know they're gone, but you keep them present in your heart and mind—even as you move forward with your life. They become part of your psychological family.

No Right Way to Grieve

Before I go any further, I need to clarify that "normal grief" does not in any way mean there's one right way to grieve. Rather, it means that while grief reveals itself differently in different cultures and communities, it should not immobilize anyone for years. Grieving normally, in a healthy way, means we both carry our sadness and eventually function again, taking care of ourselves and others, and finding some pleasure in life again.

In the epigraph at the head of this chapter, Freud defined normal grief as "grave departures from the normal attitude towards life," but one that would not need medical treatment. A bit vague. However, he differentiated between mourning, what he considered ordinary or normal grief, and melancholia, what is now considered depression. Unfortunately, today, that early focus on normal grief has been nearly lost in a sea of pathologies with an emphasis on grief as illness.

Yet I am often asked, "Is this normal?", referring to reactions and behaviors after a loss. Sometimes the answer is yes and sometimes no. Often the answer lies somewhere in between. It depends on how long the concerning behavior or feelings have been going on. With millions of deaths worldwide from the ongoing pandemic, we need to know what is considered normal grief and what requires professional help.

What Is Normal Grief?

Normal grief is the natural and expected response of deep sorrow and pain after losing someone or something you love. While there are cultural and contextual differences, there's no one right way to grieve.

With normal grief, many of the signs are similar to those of a major depression—feelings of emptiness, fatigue, perhaps loss of appetite, inability to sleep, inability to feel pleasure, and sometimes guilt—but there are two essential signs that your grief is normal. First, such symptoms become less intense over weeks and months, and second, you do not have feelings of worthlessness and self-loathing.

Ordinarily, after several weeks or a few months, we can resume work and daily life again, but often at a lower level, and with a weariness we didn't have before the loss. This lack of energy after a major loss is typical. The sadness of loss comes and goes in something like waves, what researchers call "oscillations." Over time, however, these waves of sadness happen less often. While the grief may never stop completely, the upside is that these times of sadness no longer dominate. We can experience some pleasure again.

When Professional Help Is Needed

There are times, however, when grief is not normal and professional or medical help is needed. If you're thinking your life isn't worth living, hating yourself, abusing alcohol or drugs, no longer taking care of yourself, feeling helpless or hopeless, wishing you had died along with your loved one, or thinking about suicide, seek professional help immediately. These symptoms are life threatening. Also seek professional help if after several months or a year, your grief remains so intense that it still impairs your daily functioning. Again, if you're thinking about suicide, immediately tell someone you trust; seek professional therapy; or call the National Suicide Prevention Lifeline, 1-800-273-8255, toll free.

■ ■ ■

Being quiet about my grief after Eddie died didn't mean I was done with it; rather, in the cultural context of my Swiss American family and community, it meant that we were expected to grieve more quietly. Yet, decades later, when a phone call came to my university office informing me that my sister, Ellie, had died, a sound came out of me that I had never heard before—a primal wail that must have frightened nearby staff and students. The department chair rushed out of his office and, realizing what happened, tried to comfort me. Class was over, and I took the next plane south.

As with my little brother, I will always remember my older sister, Ellie. She was livelier and more social than I. She wore bright colors, big jewelry, and lots of perfume. I think of her every time I see a red dress in a store window. I wear one of her rings still, given to me because it was the most modest ring she had. I still see her now in the faces of her children and grandchildren. She would be so proud of them. I am proud of them for her.

As time went on, there were other losses: the deaths of my good friends, Paula and Nick; the divorce from Ken, who was my high school sweetheart and the father of my children; the deaths of my good Swiss parents, Verena and Paul; and since then, the death of my young son-in-law, Mike, from pancreatic cancer; plus the loss of other friends too numerous to name. And then during the pandemic, the death of my husband, the love of my life, who died of a stroke.

During the pandemic, there were more losses. Aside from the ambiguous losses of freedom to be with friends and family, to travel and work in my usual way, there was the death of Lotte, my Swiss first cousin; my friend and colleague, Karen, with whom I wrote about clinical issues; and Lorraine, my friend and colleague with whom I worked after 9/11 with New York's labor union families. Then a colleague from suicide, and then my poet friend, Carol, from Alzheimer's disease. She was like a sister to me.

After Eddie's death, was I ever happy again? Yes. I have had a wonderful life. But the price we pay for loving others is the pain of loss and grief. It is also the price we pay for living a long life. I know now, in my late 80s, that the people in my life whom I loved, who loved me, who taught me, and who are now gone—all remain part of who I am and always will be as long as memory holds.

■ ■ ■

In my training as a family therapist, I read the writings of experts who wrote academically about grief, but I enjoyed even more reading their personal writings. There, they tended to show a humanity I did not see in their formal writings where focus was on *detachment* or finishing one's grief. In 1996, a major challenge came in a book called *Continuing Bonds*. It was compiled by Klass and colleagues who proposed that after death, bonds continued. I sensed they too were searching for meaning. To understand normal grief, and to keep a deceased loved one present in some symbolic way, we take a look back to some personal writings of the experts.

The Personal and the Professional

Sigmund Freud

In 1920, after Freud's beloved daughter, Sophie, died during the lingering Spanish flu pandemic, Freud revealed an enduring bond to her. When a patient expressed her condolences to Freud about Sophie's untimely death (she was only 27), he responded by pulling a locket on a chain from his vest pocket, patted it, and said, "She is here." Whether the locket contained a lock of her hair or her photo or even nothing at all, we don't know, but it was apparently for him a symbol of his daughter's presence. For Freud, there was no closure here; he kept his daughter symbolically present even after her death. His actions reflected a continuous bond, not closure.

In 1923, after the death of his favorite grandson, Heinele (Sophie's son), Freud wrote a revealing letter, this time to his colleague Ludwig Binswanger. In it, he wrote that mourning could never be fully resolved. A few years later, when Binswanger's own son died, Freud wrote to him about how it should be:

> *Although we know after such a loss the acute state of mourning will subside, we also know we shall remain inconsolable and will never find a substitute. No matter what may fill the gap, even if it be filled completely, it nevertheless remains something else. And this is how it should be, it is the only way of perpetuating that love which we do not want to relinquish.*

I find comfort in those lines. After the loss of both his beloved daughter and his grandson, and as he grew older, it appears that Freud shifted his thoughts, at least personally, to the idea of continuing bonds, an idea more consistent with today's research findings. After years of suffering from mouth cancer and knowing his time was now limited, Freud wrote to his good friend, Marie Bonaparte: . . . "I hope you will soon console yourself over my death and let me go on living in your friendly recollections—the only kind of limited immortality I recognize." Freud seemed to be hoping that when he dies, his good friend will keep him present in her mind and memory instead of seeking closure. I find comfort in these lines, too.

For me professionally, perhaps Freud's message that rings most true appears in an obscure essay written when he was younger, after a summertime walk in the mountains with two friends, one probably the poet Rainer Maria Rilke. Back then, Freud's ideas were more erudite, but the lines I value are these: "Mourning over the loss of something that we have loved or admired seems so natural to the layman that he regards it as self-evident. But to psychologists, mourning is a great riddle." Indeed. And the riddle continues. But now, through research, we listen to more laypeople and thus have more data about what's normal and what's not.

Elisabeth Kübler-Ross

Personal views are also found in the writings of Elisabeth Kübler-Ross, the veritable godmother of the five stages of *dying*, which, against her intention, became the five stages of grief. While her last two books reveal a change in her thinking, people are stuck on her early thinking about the five stages of grief. One must read those last books to get her updates, but here is a summary.

After a series of debilitating strokes, and shortly before she died, Kübler-Ross called her own process of dying a "nightmare." She acknowledged the changing face of grief today and regretted that her ideas were so misunderstood. In her last book, she wrote that her views had changed. When asked how long it took to get through the five stages, she wrote, "Grief is not just a series of events, stages, or timelines. Our society places enormous pressure on us to get over loss, to get through the grief."

Up to her last days, Elisabeth Kübler-Ross continued to correct the misuse of her five stages: "They were never meant to help tuck messy emotions into neat packages. The five stages—denial, anger, bargaining, depression, and acceptance—are part of the framework that makes up our learning to live with the one we lost. . . . But they are not stops on some linear timeline in grief."

Approaching the end of her life, Dr. Kübler-Ross wrote of her personal focus on acceptance, because she was frustrated and impatient with the years she lingered with paralysis. Just before her death, she wrote, "Acceptance is a process that we experience, not a final stage with an end point." She reiterated that she meant the five stages for the dying, not for the mourners, but then revealed her frustration and anger with her own dying process. Near the end, she wrote:

> *Being ill for nine years has forced me to learn patience. . . . I know death is close, but not quite yet. I lie here like so many people over the years, in a bed surrounded by flowers and looking out a big window. A room not much different from that first good death I saw. These last years have been like being stuck on a runway, not allowed to die and leave this earth, but not allowed to go back to the gate and fully live.*

My empathy for Kübler-Ross grew as I read these almost last words. We both had Swiss parents, so I had followed her career closely. I did not agree with her five linear stages, and yet they caught on with the public. Perhaps that was because the five neat stages made grief look as if it could be finished step by step. But alas, no. It doesn't work that way, as she herself said in her last days.

She ends her last book with a final message to us:

> *The process of dying when it is prolonged like mine is a nightmare. I have struggled with the constant pain and*

paralysis. After many years of total independence, it is a difficult state of being. It has been a long nine years since my stroke, and I am anxious to die—graduate as I call it. I now know that the purpose of my life is more than these stages. . . . It is not just about knowing the stages. It is not just about the life lost but also the life lived. . . . I am so much more than five stages. And so are you.

Indeed, she did much more. Elisabeth Kübler-Ross gave us all a major gift—not the five stages, but the global hospice movement. We will all benefit from her work at the end of our lives, but for now, let's heed her important last words.

Viktor Frankl

Finally, there was Viktor Frankl, whose writings helped me understand my own losses. An Austrian psychiatrist and concentration camp survivor from The World War II Holocaust, his ideas about the ongoing presence of lost loved ones, as opposed to closure, moved me. Early on, his focus on the search for meaning made sense to me and is now supported by research affirming that we can live with loss if we find some meaning in it. He personally found meaning enough to survive amid death and suffering, by keeping his beloved wife present in his mind. From the misery of the concentration camp, Frankl wrote:

My mind still clung to the image of my wife. A thought crossed my mind: I didn't even know if she were still alive. I knew only one thing—which I have learned well by now:

Love goes very far beyond the physical person of the beloved. It finds its deepest meaning in [their] spiritual being, [their] inner self. Whether or not [she] is actually present, whether or not [she] is still alive at all, ceases somehow to be of importance.

Separated within the same concentration camp from his young wife, Frankl had no way of knowing if she was still alive and, like a mantra for survival and the search for meaning, he repeated:

My mind clung to my wife's image, imagining it with an uncanny acuteness. I heard her answering me, saw her smile, her frank and encouraging look. Real or not, her look was then more luminous than the sun, which was beginning to rise. A thought transfixed me: for the first time in my life I saw the truth, as it is set into song by so many poets, proclaimed as the final wisdom by so many thinkers. The truth—that love is the ultimate and the highest goal to which [people] can aspire. Then I grasped the meaning of the greatest secret that human poetry and human thought and belief have to impart: The salvation of [human beings] is through love and in love. I understood how a [person] who has nothing left in this world still may know bliss, be it only for a brief moment, in the contemplation of [one's] beloved.

Powerful words! I am comforted by Viktor Frankl still today, knowing that one can find meaning even in suffering.

I hope you can find that, too. Continued ties to loved ones lost can comfort us in times of suffering.

This idea that the absent can be present to comfort us in troubled times has for eons been the stuff of poetry, plays, and literature. From *Antigone*, to the *Nibelungenlied*, to the *Ring* cycle, to *The Lord of the Rings*, to the Harry Potter series, and many more, the stories that keep us interested are stories about loss and its ambiguity. The human search for meaning in loss is universal and in the stories of every culture.

In the end, the most important point is that grief should not always be considered a disorder, especially when it is the context around the mourner that is disordered. It's understandable to feel weary and sad after what many experienced during the pandemic and its fellow stressors—racism, politics, poverty, food shortages, loss of income, family violence, suicides, and home-grown terrorism. Surely, there will be no closure on the mountain of losses caused by the pandemic, but now, we must try to find meaning in them. Perhaps that meaning lies in working for change.

■ ■ ■

I end this chapter now on a personal note about grief. For me, losing my husband of 32 years has been a deep sadness, for some reason especially in the morning. I also felt angry about the amount of paperwork required. It took me by surprise. The business of death, I called it. To feel both anger and sorrow at the same time was extremely distressing, but now that most of that paperwork is done, I am more at peace with my sorrow.

CHAPTER 9

LOSS AND CHANGE

Not everything that is faced can be changed; but
nothing can be changed until it is faced.
     —James Baldwin, "As Much Truth as One Can Bear"

L oss and change are inevitably linked. After loss, there is
       change, and those changes create more loss. Change cre-
       ates stress because it's an alteration in a steady state—
doing something different or doing something in a different
way. It is in times like this, when we feel unmoored from so
many losses, that change is needed to find stability.

I learned about the paradox of change from psychiatrist
Carl Whitaker. He began with a question: "What makes us
change?" He then went on to describe a therapy session in
which he said, "Nobody was up to anything in that hour, and
it changed everything." He went on, "Unless we get past the
tricks, there is little change that will happen in the clients."

Always vague and paradoxical, Whitaker never liked planned
strategies. He preferred spontaneity; he valued the experien-

tial, not the discussion about it. Whitaker was for me the best teacher, an antithesis to all I had been. He gave me the courage to change. To be less decisive; to be more flexible. To take a risk.

"What makes us change?" he asked again. "Not an education—otherwise all educated people would be integrated and mature. Is it support? No, that's an illusion you get used to, like having a mother who always cooks for you. It's infantilizing." And then, a third time: "What really makes us change? Interaction between the therapist and family—and *radiation*."

What? Really? Did I hear wrong? Or was his last word an intentional absurdity? As a doctoral student, I had worked with Dr. Whitaker as his cotherapist for several years and had seen this kind of absurdity before in his clinical sessions. Now, he was purposely creating confusion, throwing us off balance, so we might open ourselves to change. The shift comes when we least expect it.

So, what does bring about change? Contrary to what my professor thought, knowing more about it can also help. There are two kinds of change: first order and second order. *First-order change* means pushing harder on what you have been doing. It's more of the same, but putting more energy into it. *Second-order change* is what is now called thinking outside the box, taking a new direction.

When cars all had stick shifts, we said first-order change was pushing down harder on the gas pedal to drive a car up a steep hill, but it killed the motor and didn't work—whereas second-order change was shifting into a lower gear to get more power to get up the hill. Second-order change is considered transformation for survival.

Pushing ahead during a deadly pandemic, for example, living life the way one always did, ignoring the danger, avoiding new information, was first-order change—and dangerous. On the other hand, most of us used second-order change by deciding to do something different—staying home; wearing a mask; social distancing; using Zoom online for family gatherings, funerals, introducing a new baby, and everything in between. This was not an easy shift from our usual way of getting together, but necessary for the common good.

I use the term "shift" intentionally to illustrate change, but you will have to imagine a car that requires manual shifting for this metaphor to work. Sometimes, especially when there's high stress, one has to shift gears and do something systemically different to make the grade. While our personal shifting of gears can happen in isolation, it's more easily achieved in discussion with others, peers who are experiencing losses similar to yours, or a therapist. Also, talk about the changes you are considering with your partner or a friend. If you have kids, include them. They need to know what changes are coming.

Changing after loss is risky but eventually worth trying. When a family member dies or is ambiguously lost, the way you lived before may no longer work. When a pandemic happens, life is surely no longer as it was. To help in deciding what to change or not change, I make a list of the costs and benefits of changing; and then make another list—the costs and benefits of not changing. While this is a cognitive task, both cognitive and experiential approaches can help us make the difficult decisions about changing.

In this process, it's important to balance continuity with change. Continuity means keeping something the same as it was before your loss. Even something small would do. A bit of familiarity after a loss gives you the courage to risk the changes you need to make. You read a story to your child that your parent read to you; you wear the shirt of someone now gone while you study; you bake something they liked to remind you of them.

■ ■ ■

During the pandemic, there was and still is considerable resistance to change, for example, regarding vaccinations. Surprisingly, this is still a political issue, hot enough to start fights. This resistance is hard to understand as scientists have proved that vaccinations prevent the spread of this deadly virus and its variants. But resisters and pandemic deniers are apparently not thinking about others; they are thinking about protecting their own freedom to do as they please. Individualism wins out over caring about the community. Of course, a danger, like a virus—or climate change—is easy to deny, especially by those who don't believe in science, or by those who don't have access to reliable information.

The reason why many of us had trouble changing during the pandemic wasn't just due to the invisibility of the virus or to the many ambiguous losses we endured. It was likely because change is stressful; it makes us feel uncomfortable. It erodes our status quo and thus creates more ambiguity. We don't like to give up our routines and habits. But remember the smoking problem, when nearly everyone was smoking in public places? To the surprise of many, our entire nation changed on that one. Whether it was due to widespread education or the personal losses of loved ones who died from cancer, no-smoking rules were eventually accepted, saving the lives of many. In situations today when some resist change—like continuing to deny the pandemic, the need to get vaccinated, as well as the Holocaust and the outcomes of the Civil War and the 2020 presidential election—there is need for all of us to shift into a different gear.

It is in times of absurdity, when people are unmoored, that positive change is possible. History shows us this pattern in this list of large-scale losses and the changes that followed, often for the better:

- The bubonic plague, 1346–1353, which killed about half of Europe's population, was followed by the Renaissance, with new ideas about art and science.
- World War I, 1914–1918, and the flu epidemic of 1917–1918, which sickened one-third of the world's population (my father included) with at least 50 million deaths worldwide and about 675,000 deaths in the United States alone. What followed was the prosperous Roaring 20s, with advances in technology—telephones, radios, and the automobile. The women's suffrage movement reignited and continued until 1920 when women won the right to vote. (Note that while in theory all women won the right to vote with the Nineteenth Amendment, in practice most Black women were prevented from voting until the Voting Rights Act was passed in 1965.)

- World War II, 1939–1945, and the polio epidemic of the 1950s were followed by the turmoil and violence of the civil rights movement from 1954 to 1968 and beyond.
- The late 1960s and all of the 1970s saw demonstrations and marches for liberation movements of gender and sexual minorities, and Indigenous peoples, all demanding the change of laws that discriminated against them. While many changes were made, there is much left to do.
- The 1980s: More stability, yet with spectacular advances in technology—the Apple computer, Microsoft Windows, DNA fingerprinting, Voyager probes, and Pac-Man. At the same time, it was the height of the AIDS epidemic.
- The 1990s: The Rodney King police beating, and his famous response, "People, I just want to say, you know, can we all get along? Can we get along?" Riots in Los Angeles followed, but the needed changes in the Los Angeles Police Department came slowly, nearly a decade later, and only after the federal government got involved.
- 2000–2010: Increase in riots and demonstrations again, still about police killings, but now also about environmental issues such as pipelines.
- 2010–2019: The Defense of Marriage Act (DOMA) was declared unconstitutional in 2013, opening the path to federal recognition of same-sex marriage. In 2018, Greta Thunberg represented an escalation of the climate change movement among the younger generations.
- 2020: The year of the COVID-19 pandemic and George Floyd's murder; massive unrest and worldwide demonstrations in support of Black Lives Matter.

- 2021: On January 6, 2021, the violent invasion of the U.S. Capitol by insurrectionists aiming to negate the outcome of the presidential election, execute the vice president and other lawmakers—and destroy essential democratic processes. On January 20, President Joe Biden, amid a pandemic and thousands of troops protecting the capital and him, was sworn in as the 46th president of the United States. He vowed to heal the divide in our nation and serve all people, even those who did not vote for him. Kamala Harris, the newly-elected vice president, broke several glass ceilings— the first woman, first Black, and first Asian American to be elected vice president of the United States of America. Juneteenth (June 19), commemorating the end of slavery for the entire United States, is made a national holiday.

This historical pattern of turmoil followed by change reminds us that loss begets change, and change begets disorder and stress, and they beget change again. We are in that period of change now. On the basis of history, I predict that after this pandemic, the murder of George Floyd by a policeman, and the insurrection of 2021, we will be in for some massive changes. May these changes be for the good of all. This has not always been the case. Not all lives have mattered, and they must. There are gross inequities and disparities in our nation, especially for people of color, and still for women. If there is any good that will come out of the COVID-19 pandemic, it's that it revealed that what we thought was fixed was not. The civil rights laws enacted in the 1960s were a step in the right direction but not enough.

For more change to happen, we need to shift gears—how we think, what we do, how we heal from the pandemic's losses. Above all, we need to increase our tolerance for ambiguity and temper our absolute thinking. We may have learned how to do that during our quarantining because we had to; living life in a new way, doing something we did not choose to do. It was both a new adventure and a tragic time.

■ ■ ■

I no longer drive a car with a stick shift, but I still value the metaphor of shifting gears. It illustrates systemic change. It reminds me to give up pushing harder, as I have a tendency to do just that. Doing the same thing, but pushing harder, is not always useful for me, especially now. To shift gears, I take a break, reassess the situation, listen to some music, go for a walk, talk with a friend or my kids and grandkids, and ponder how to proceed. While I had to change course when the pandemic hit in early 2020, I am resisting further change now, so soon after my husband's death. With so great a loss, I need some continuity to hold on to. Further changes are delayed but will eventually come.

Surely, with all these clear and ambiguous losses that happened during the pandemic, we can't expect to go back to the *normal* we had. Things change whether we want them to or not. What we need, however, is change that is kind to us. Yet, Eastern thinkers would not agree. We should not expect to be rewarded for our suffering. Instead, we should find meaning in the pain of our loss and grow from that suffering.

Change is always stressful, but not always bad. Growth

and maturity can follow. But as James Baldwin wrote, in 1962, "Nothing can be changed until it is faced." While we can't change the horror of all that happened during the 2020–2021 pandemic, we must change to make life safer and better for everyone in the human family. Paradoxically, being isolated during the pandemic allowed me to see this more clearly. There was time for reflection.

Reflections

During the time of the pandemic, life became a constancy of loss and uncertainty. So many deaths, so many obscure losses, harder to notice, but still causing grief and anxiety. As family members and close friends were physically cut off from one another, each became an ambiguous loss to the other. Not only did we lose their company, but we also lost our sense of security.

For me, in Minneapolis, anxiety was constant because there was political unrest. Outside my window, in the spring of 2020, I saw thousands of people marching peacefully in protest of police brutality. When they reached the I-35W bridge across the Mississippi River, a semi-truck driver, not knowing the road was closed, almost ran into the marchers. Miraculously, no marchers were hurt. But later, to increase my anxiety even more, I saw what looked like soldiers posted in front of my building where I was looking out of the window.

Back then, I was struggling to take in all that was happening at once—the danger of a deadly virus, the huge demonstrations set off by the murder of George Floyd—and caring for my increasingly ill husband. That was the summer of 2020—a social upheaval, a paradigm shift, a tipping point. Perhaps all three. There will be no closure on this time. Relief, yes, but no ending. It felt more like a beginning of change. And it was.

Since then, I have been to the site of George Floyd's murder twice, once shortly after his death and then again, after my husband's death. Back then it was a somber place. In a formerly busy intersection, the grocery store and shops were still there, but no traffic was allowed. Instead, there were blankets of flowers everywhere; a large mural of George Floyd, and others on the plywood used to board up nearby shop windows; and posters on every lamppost. Among the flowers, there was a special place, an outline of Mr. Floyd's body on the pavement, surrounded by candles and fresh flowers, and more amazing artwork. Nearby there was and still is a Say Their Names Cemetery, where 100 Black Americans who died at the hands of law enforcement are each named on a headstone. I was stunned to see how many there were. I saw it all. I learned; I took it in. In the silence of that place, I felt sadness and anger and resolve for change.

But what kind of change? Systemic change would require a shift in our ways of thinking, which is what this book is about. Just like a family in trouble—and we are as a nation in trouble. In order to change, we must see our problems, face them, and then act to bring about real change for the well-being of everyone. We must shift gears and use our amazing capacity to fix what sorely needs fixing.

■ ■ ■

Hopefully, you will find some meaning and new hope in what you have lost during this time of loss and change. Instead of closure, balance your sadness and grief with some joy and laughter. As you venture out into the world in a new way now, know that your bonds to those you lost can continue. No need to forget. No need for closure. Honor what you had and move forward. Tell your story to the next generation, but include your strengths as well as your sorrows, your resilience as well as your despair. Keep going. The slow climb back to some semblance of normalcy will not be easy, but you can do it with the support of others and a boost in your tolerance for ambiguity. To ease your anxiety, embrace the paradox of absence and presence and use both/and thinking.

But first, reflect on your own losses. Ask yourself questions. What does your loss mean to you? Was it clear or ambiguous? Was it unexpected or predictable? Did any others have a similar loss at the same time? If so, did you connect with them? Do you now have enough power and mastery to change? Can you imagine some new hopes and dreams now, or is it too soon? Once you find meaning and new purpose in your life, you will also find some new hope.

In the end, your main benefit in any time of adversity is that you can discover your resiliency; that you are stronger than you thought; that you can withstand long-term hardship and unprecedented loss; that even if sometimes you feel anger or despair, you can take a break, talk with someone, nurture yourself, and when ready, carry on again.

With remarkable resilience, we find ways to cope with loss; sometimes with grit or with humor; other times with a mixture of sadness, rage, and resentment. You may have had some strange responses to your losses, but likely they were normal for these abnormal times. Your safety and health depended on changing your ways, and most of you did so willingly. Give yourselves a pat on the back. But tell both sides of the story to the next generation. Loss is both awful and enlightening.

And now, how do I end a book about ambiguity and no closure? "End it in midsentence," my grandson said. True, there's no final conclusion to what I've written. Make your own sense of it. Along the way, try to find some meaning and new hope in your life. Let your tolerance for ambiguity grow, for therein lies the resilience to help us live with loss—past, present, and future. Few losses are entirely clear, and none need closure.

I leave it at that. More to come? Maybe. Maybe not.

Afterword

If you are reading this, you have managed to survive this epic time of great suffering and loss. We are changed by what we have seen and heard. Writing this book therefore was like writing on shifting sands. Life kept changing with each onslaught of death. Ambiguous losses continued to create confusion about what was real and what was not. Multiple crises about voting and vaccines merged into hostilities that intensified. Many of you discovered you were more resilient than you thought, but the unrest continued and still worries us today. So does the deadly virus—now with mutations. There will be no closure on this pandemic time, but hopefully, the viruses as well as the hostilities will become less intense.

Since I finished the book, there are some updates I want to share with you; they are relevant to the need for us all to see, remember, work on what is still unjust—and to stop using the term "closure" because it impedes our progress.

The first update is about January 6, 2021, when mobs of insurrectionists, fueled by lies, stormed our nation's capital because they wouldn't accept the outcome of the 2020 presidential election. Lawmakers and the vice president were threatened, five people died, many were hurt. Immense damage was done to the Capitol building, costing over $30 million to repair. As of now, more than 570 defendants have been charged.

While we are still reeling from this uprising, vaccinations are beginning to bring relief and new hope to a weary population. Yet, sadly, the unrest, the mutations, and the inequities in healthcare systems around the world continued. No closure here, either.

■ ■ ■

In early 2021, there was the trial of Derek Chauvin, accused of murdering George Floyd nearly a year before. On April 20, 2021, an anxious crowd and worldwide press gathered in front of the Hennepin County Courthouse in Minneapolis to hear the jury's verdict. After about 10 hours of deliberation, it was announced, "Guilty, guilty, guilty." On all three counts of murder and manslaughter, the jurors unanimously found this white policeman guilty of unjustly killing a Black man. As the jury results were announced, I was watching television and was surprised by the immediate response—the tension in the crowd yielded, not to elation, but to a surprising hush with some tears and sighs of relief. At that moment, I saw grief mixed with joy. It was not yet justice, but accountability, a step in the right direction. No closure, just a beginning.

Finally, there is an update that brought me honor and joy. On June 11, 2021, Darnella Frazier, whose video recording of

George Floyd's murder went around the world, was awarded a Pulitzer Prize citation for citizen journalism. I applaud, especially, such young people. They are not afraid of change; they seek it. In them, I see possibilities for less prejudice and more equality in our vastly diverse national family. What Darnella Frazier did was make us *see* that the struggle for justice is far from over. But due to her citizen journalism, that struggle took a leap forward.

While I see some good things happening now, racial disparities continue to exist in COVID-19 death tolls, in the availability of health care, food, housing, economic opportunities, and the technology and internet access needed for home schooling and paid work. As protestor Simone Hunter said, "It's not just about George Floyd. It's about all the unseen sh*t where we *don't* have the video."

■ ■ ■

I wrote this book because Americans really like the term "closure"; they say things like: The parents will have closure once their child's body is found; without a funeral, a widow can have no closure; or now that the murderer has gone to prison or been executed, the family has closure. Not so! The myth is that healthy people find closure, but the truth is that resilient people live well without it.

Divided as we are, I see renewed energy in the will of many to do the right thing, not just for themselves, but for the survival of the human family. Continued thinking about the absolute of closure blocks not only our self-understanding but also the ability to empathize with the suffering of others. If we believe that people experiencing loss should just get over it, then we have to shut down our own ability to feel—and we are terribly alone.

May we have the courage and flexibility to change; may the pandemic virus and its variants become manageable, less deadly. May more people pay attention to facts, get vaccinated, and have their children vaccinated. And finally, may those of us whose loved ones died during this time never be told again that we need to find closure.

Notes

Preface

xvii *The rest is history.*

See Ambiguous Loss, https://www.ambiguousloss.com.

Chapter 1: Ambiguous Loss

3 *Ambiguous losses then lead to a disenfranchised grief because others do not see the loss as credible and worthy of grief.*

Some examples of disenfranchised grief include loss of a pet, miscarriage, loss of friend or lover, or loss of a limb (Doka, 2002).

Doka, K. (2002). *Disenfranchised grief: New directions, challenges, and strategies for practice.* Research Press.

7 *If such losses make you feel helpless, hopeless, or self-loathing, seek professional therapy.*

To find a therapist, see American Association for Marriage and Family Therapy (AAMFT) at https://aamft.org/Directories/Find_a_Therapist.aspx and the American Psychological Association (APA) at https://locator.apa.org/.

7 *First, to lower your stress and anxiety during confusing times, increase your tolerance for ambiguity.*

Researchers have developed a Tolerance for Ambiguity Scale. Examples of higher tolerance for ambiguity tend to reflect being comfortable with the unfamiliar and liking it (Herman et al., 2010).

Herman, J. L., Stevens, M. J., Bird, A., Mendenhall, M., & Oddou, G. (2010). The Tolerance for Ambiguity Scale: Towards a more refined mea-

121

sure for international management research. *International Journal of Intercultural Relations*, 34, 58–65. https://doi.org/10.1016/j.ijintrel.2009.09.004

9   *"What you are experiencing is ambiguous loss; it is the most difficult loss because it defies resolution. This is not your fault. The problem is the ambiguity, not you. It can traumatize." With this, the work begins.*

In large disasters, this approach was used to help families of the missing in New York, Kosovo, Ukraine, Japan, Australia, Mexico, Zurich, Geneva, New York, and more. Researchers and clinicians are now using the ambiguous loss theory globally to understand various kinds of ambiguous losses. The coronavirus pandemic offers a large-scale use of this lens, just as 9/11 did in New York City and the 3/11 earthquake and tsunami did in Japan, and after many hurricanes, fires, and floods.

Chapter 2: The Myth of Closure

19   *"Because in the end, I actually have NO control over other people's destinies, but I can continue to accept and grow in mine."*

Personal communication; also see Johnson (2015).

Johnson, S. M. (2015). *Life is beautiful: How a lost girl became a true, confident child of God*. Morgan James.

Chapter 3: Racism as Unresolved Loss

29   *As a result, the stress and trauma suffered by Black people as well as all people of color continue today.*

Currently, "a disproportionate number of African American youth experience childhood adversity" (Brown & Coker, p. 286) and ambiguous losses, including parental incarceration, drug use, and divorce, while also "navigating racial discrimination" (p. 286). Black researchers say that "ambiguous loss theory offers a conceptual framework to understand" (p. 286) the stressful experiences of "losses of relationships, stability, and social validation due to parental behaviors" (p. 286) and that informed interventions are needed to help adolescents cope with these ambiguous losses. As a result, psychoeducational groups have been formed for female African American adolescents "experiencing ambiguous loss that aims to promote resilience and coping" (p. 286) after the loss rather than closure. This reflects the interventions we created with labor union families after 9/11 in New York City (Boss et al., 2003), with families in Japan (Boss & Ishii, 2015), Eastern Europe, Mexico, and what the International Committee of the Red Cross does with families experiencing the stress of ambiguous loss around the world (ICRC, 2013).

Boss, P., Beaulieu, L., Wieling, E., Turner, W., & LaCruz, S. (2003). Healing loss, ambiguity, and trauma: A community-based intervention with families of union workers missing after the 9/11 attack in New York City. *Journal of Marital and Family Therapy*, 29(4), 455– 467. https://doi .org/10.1111/j.1752-0606.2003.tb01688.x

Boss, P., & Ishii, C. (2015). Trauma and ambiguous loss: The lingering presence of the physically absent. In K. E. Cherry (Ed.), *Traumatic stress and long-term recovery* (pp. 271–289). Springer International. https://doi .org/10.1007/978-3-319-18866-9

Brown, E. C., & Coker, A. D. (2019). Promoting the resiliency of African American teens experiencing ambiguous loss. *Journal for Specialists in Group Work*, 44(4), 286–299. https://doi.org/10.1080/01933922.2019.1 669751

ICRC. (2013). *Accompanying the families of missing persons.* International Committee of the Red Cross. https://www.icrc.org/en/publica-tion/4110-accompanying-families-missing-persons-practical-handbook

30 *Their pain is remembered today in the bodies and minds of their descendants, but also for those of us without that history in books, films, and programs like* Finding Your Roots, *all of which reveal some of those family patterns of suffering and also resilience.*

A PBS series hosted by historian Henry Louis Gates Jr., who, with genealogists, traces the family trees of celebrities.

31 *But there are differing views about how this happens.*

Epigenetics researchers find that on the basis of memory and learning, there is a harmful impact of racism on African Americans' physical health and the health of their offspring. Others say it is learned behavior.

31 *We know from past studies of Holocaust mothers and their children that the effects of trauma can be passed down from mother to child.*

Regarding trauma and its transmission across generations,

researchers found that Holocaust survivors did parent differently, holding the secret of their trauma from their children, while their children sensed their withdrawal. (See Dashorst et al. 2019.)

Dashorst, P., Mooren, T. M., Kleber, R. J., de Jong, P. J., & Huntjens, R. J. (2019). Intergenerational consequences of the Holocaust on offspring mental health: A systematic review of associated factors and mechanisms. *European Journal of Psychotraumatology*, 10(1), 1654065. https://doi .org/10 .1080/20008198.2019.1654065

32   *Meanwhile, from a more social-psychological perspective, Joy DeGruy proposes a theory of post-traumatic slave syndrome.*

What Native Americans call a "soul wound" (Duran, 2006) may also be an epigenetic wound passed across the generations.

Duran, E. (2006). *Healing the soul wound: Counseling with American Indians and other Native peoples.* Teachers College Press.

32   *Second, I am wary of adapting mental illness terms (such as 'disorder' or 'syndrome') for people who have been traumatized by an outside force.*

Many veterans prefer the term "PTS" instead of "PTSD" as they do not see it as *their* disorder.

Also see Boss and Ishii (2015), Braga et al. (2012), Crist (2017), DeAngelis (2019), and Kazan (2018).

Boss, P., & Ishii, C. (2015). Trauma and ambiguous loss: The lingering presence of the physically absent. In K. E. Cherry (Ed.), *Traumatic stress and long-term recovery* (pp. 271–289). Springer International. https://doi. org/10.1007/978-3-319-18866-9

Braga, L. L., Mello, M. F., & Fiks, J. P. (2012). Transgenerational transmission of trauma and resilience: A qualitative study with Brazilian offspring of Holocaust survivors. *BMC Psychiatry*, 12(134). https://doi. org/10.1186/1471-244X-12-134

Crist, C. (2017, January 6). *Holocaust survivors remember with resilience.* Reuters. https://www.reuters.com/article/us-health-trauma-resilience/holo caust-survivors-remember-with-resilience-idUSKBN14Q21H

DeAngelis, T. (2019). The legacy of trauma. *Monitor on Psychology*, 50(2) 36. https://www.apa.org/monitor/2019/02/legacy-trauma

Kazan, O. (2018, October 16). Inherited trauma shapes your health.

The Atlantic. https://www.theatlantic.com/health/archive/2018/10/trauma
-inherited-generations/573055/

34   *This courageous young woman's video was seen around the world and
    opened the eyes of millions of people, including me.*

In December 2020, a surprised Darnella Frazier was awarded
the prestigious Benenson Courage Award from PEN America for
recording the death of George Floyd with a cell phone. It was
presented to her virtually by Oscar winning director Spike Lee
(Walsh, 2021). Then, in June 2021, Darnella received a special
citation from the Pulitzer Board for her recording (Hernandez,
2021).

Hernandez, J. (2021, June 11). *Darnella Frazier, who filmed George
Floyd's murder, wins an honorary Pulitzer.* NPR *News.* https://www.npr.
org/2021/06/11/1005601724/darnella-frazierteen-who-filmed-george-floyds
-murder-wins-pulitzer-prize-citati

Walsh, P. (2021, March 12). For first time, Minneapolis teen opens up
about her viral George Floyd arrest video. *Star Tribune.* https://www.star
tribune.com/for-first-time-minneapolis-teen-opens-up-about-her-viral-
george-floyd-arrest-video/600033586/

34   *My colleague in family therapy, Elaine Pinderhughes, was one of the
    first to teach me that historical context matters for human develop-
    ment and that being traumatized instead of nurtured will affect not
    only children, but their offspring as well.*

Elaine Pinderhughes' chapter entitled "The Multigenerational
Transmission of Loss and Trauma: The African American Experience," in Walsh & McGoldrick (2004), is prescient and powerful,
as she is the pioneer in writing about the cross-generational transmission of trauma for Black families, from slavery to now.

Pinderhughes, E. (2004). The multigenerational transmission of loss
and trauma: The African-American experience. In F. Walsh & M. McGoldrick (Eds.), *Living beyond loss: Death in the family* (2nd ed., pp. 161– 181).
W. W. Norton.

Walsh, F., & McGoldrick, M. (Eds.). (2004). *Living beyond loss: Death
in the family* (2nd ed.). W. W. Norton.

Chapter 4: Resilience: Our Best Hope in the Face of Ambiguous Loss

39 *After near devastation, it is now flourishing as the Survivor Tree at the 9/11 Memorial.*

The tree was removed from the rubble and cared for by the Department of Parks and Recreation. In 2010, it was replanted at what is now the memorial. Out of the gnarled stumps, there were now new, smooth limbs, showing both the tree's traumatic past and its new growth. Today, the tree at the 9/11 Memorial in New York is a symbol of resilience, survival, and rebirth. For more information, see "The Survivor Tree," 9/11 Memorial and Museum, https://www.911memorial.org/visit/memorial/survivor-tree.

41 *That is, while the first studies on resilience were done with poor and homeless children in Hawaii, the problems of homelessness and poverty are avoidable. They can be ameliorated.*

Psychologist Norman Garmezy (1983) pioneered the study of resilience in children, but early on called it "competence."

Garmezy, N. (1983). Stressors of childhood. In N. Garmezy & M. Rutter (Eds.), *Stress, coping, and development in children* (pp. 43–84). McGraw-Hill.

43 *While children need to be protected, we also need to give them the opportunity to build their own resilience, sometimes allowing them to figure things out on their own.*

This does not apply to children who must too often cope on their own, for example, migrant children or children of poverty, abuse, neglect, famine, or war. They may be in danger. While many of these children may show surprising resilience, no child should have to constantly cope on their own.

Chapter 5: The Paradox of Absence and Presence

50 *He disappeared during the Troubles in Northern Ireland during the 1960s, so she was considered by others to be both a wife and not-a-wife.*

An ethnic conflict from 1968 to 1998.

50 *When her missing husband was finally found buried in a bog, she*

still had many unanswered questions, and the conflict continued. Her story of loss was without an ending.

The Ferryman was developed by Sonia Friedman Productions and premiered at the Jerwood Theatre Downstairs at the Royal Court Theatre, London, April 24, 2017. It was subsequently transferred to the Gielgud Theatre, London, on June 20, 2017, by Sonia Friedman Productions, Neal Street Productions, and Royal Court Theatre Productions with Rupert Gavin, Gavin Kalin Productions, Ron Kastner, and Tulchin Bartner Productions. The production moved to the Bernard B. Jacobs Theater on Broadway in New York City in October 2018.

50 *Someone who is sitting near us can be gone cognitively and emotionally if they have advanced dementia or are addicted to drugs or alcohol.*

As a poet writes about a psychologically absent spouse, in this case due to alcohol addiction, he is "on safari while feeding at my table" (Connolly, 2009, p. 15).

Connolly, C. (2009). Distance at close range. In *All this and more.* Nodin Press.

55 *The story about the Ferryman rowing the dead across the river Styx is an ancient one, but as I sat in a Broadway theater, watching this play, I wondered if this fear of missing loved ones not being able to rest in peace is the reason why some families, for generations, keep on searching for their missing soldiers.*

In his book *Vanished*, Wil Hylton (2013) writes about the continued search for a World War II pilot who vanished in 1944 somewhere in the Pacific.

Hylton, W. (2013). Vanished. Riverhead Books.

56 *Perhaps this is why mystery stories are so popular; they always end with a clear and perfect solution.*

Except for Kenneth Branagh's 2017 film, *Murder on the Orient Express*, which had a delightfully ambiguous ending.

Chapter 6: Both/And Thinking

65 *Today, millions of women, men, and teenagers are taking care of family members who have a terminal illness, a physical or psychological ailment, or some disability.*

An estimated 53 million Americans were caregivers for adults or children with special needs in 2020 (AARP & National Alliance for Caregiving, Caregiving in the U.S. 2020, ExecutiveSummary,p.ES-1.   https://www.caregiving.org/wpcontent/uploads/2020/08/ AARP1316_ExecSum_CaregivingintheUS_508.pdf).

Chapter 7: Six Guidelines for the Resilience to Live With Loss

69 *This is the ability to withstand the pain of loss and the anxiety of ambiguity, get up again after we've been knocked down, and grow stronger from the suffering.*

Ann Masten (2001), George Bonanno (2004, 2019), and Froma Walsh (1998) all find that we have a profound capacity for resilience and that most people live good lives along with loss and grief and do not need medical intervention after loss, but they do this by finding new layers of meaning.

Bonanno, G. A. (2004). Loss, trauma, and human resilience: Have we underestimated the human capacity to thrive after extremely aversive events? *American Psychologist*, 59(1), 20–28. https://doi.org/10.103 7/0003-066x.59.1.20

Bonanno, G. A. (2019). *The other side of sadness: What the new science for bereavement tells us about life after loss.* Basic Books. (Original work published 2009)

Masten, A. S. (2001). Ordinary magic: Resilience processes in development. *American Psychologist*, 56(3), 227–238. https://doi.org/10.1037/ 0003-066x.56.3.227

Walsh, F. (1998). *Strengthening family resilience* (2nd ed.). Guilford Press.

70 *In no particular order, as indicated by the various connecting lines in Figure 7.1 , the following guidelines can help build your resilience: finding meaning, adjusting need for mastery, reconstructing identity, normalizing ambivalence, revising attachment, and discovering new hope.*

Each guideline emerged from years of research, field work, and clinical work with families of the lost and missing, and today, from continued testing by a new generation of researchers. A full chapter is devoted to each guideline in Boss (2006).

Boss, P. (2006). *Loss, trauma, and resilience: Therapeutic work with ambiguous loss.* W. W. Norton.

72 *After my little brother died of polio, we all went door to door collecting dimes to fund research for a vaccine.*

The March of Dimes organization began in 1938 as the National Foundation for Infantile Paralysis, funding research to find a vaccine to eradicate polio. They did. In 1976, it became known as the March of Dimes Birth Defects Foundation, and in 2007, the March of Dimes Foundation (Baghdady & Maddock, 2008).

Baghdady, G., & Maddock, J. M. (2008). Marching to a different mission. *Stanford Social Innovation Review*, 60–65.

73 *Said another way, we find meaning even through suffering. Viktor Frankl found meaning in a concentration camp; Antonovksy found it in hospitals working with cancer patients.*

The search for meaning was first promoted by Viktor Frankl as a way to maintain purpose in one's life. This gave people a will to live. Researchers and clinicians now see finding meaning as necessary for normal grief and meaninglessness as a "cardinal marker of debilitating bereavement reactions across many populations" (Prigerson et al. 2009, in Neimeyer et al. 2011, pp. 11–12). Like Aaron Antonovsky's (1979, 1987) sense of coherence, Viktor Frankl said that "striving to find a meaning in one's life is the primary motivational force" (Frankl, 2006, p. 99).

Antonovsky, A. (1979). *Health, stress, and coping: New perspectives on mental and physical well-being.* Jossey-Bass.

Antonovsky, A. (1987). *Unraveling the mystery of health: How people manage stress and stay well.* Jossey-Bass.

Frankl, V. (2006). *Man's search for meaning.* Beacon Press. (Original English publication, 1959)

Neimeyer, R. A., Harris, D. L., Winokuer, H. R., & Thornton, G. F. (Eds.). (2011). *Grief and bereavement in contemporary society: Bridging research and practice.* Routledge/Taylor & Francis Group. https://doi.org/10.1080/01924788.2013.845721

Prigerson, H. G., Horowitz, M. J., Jacobs, S. C., Parkes, C. M., Aslan, M., Goodkin, K., Raphael, B., Marwit, S. J., Wortman, C., Neimeyer, R. A., Bonanno, G., Block, S. D., Kissane, D., Boelen, P., Maercker, A., Litz, B. T., Johnson, J. G., First, M. B., Maciejewski, P. K. (2009). Prolonged grief disorder: Psychometric validation of criteria proposed for *DSM-V and ICD-11. PLoS Medicine*, 10(12). https://doi.org/10.1371/journal.pmed.1000121

74 *This, however, is a privilege not everyone has. Poverty, famine, war, discrimination, or disasters, for example, can take away one's actual mastery and control. In order to know how to cope, it is useful to understand your own need for power and control now.*

Mastery was originally defined by Pearlin & Schooler (1978) and discussed in depth in Boss (2006).

Boss, P. (2006). *Loss, trauma, and resilience: Therapeutic work with ambiguous loss.* W. W. Norton.

Pearlin, L. I., & Schooler, C. (1978). The structure of coping. *Journal of Health and Social Behavior,* 19(1), 2–21. https://doi.org/10.2307/2136319

80 *In psychology, ambivalence means having conflicting feelings and emotions at the same time.*

Eugen Bleuler used the term for the first time in a lecture in 1910; see Bleuler (1910) in Boss (2006).

Bleuler, E. (1910). Vortrag über ambivalenz [Lecture on ambivalence]. *Zentralblatt für Psychoanalyse* [Central Journal for Psychoanalysis], 1, 266–268.

Boss, P. (2006). *Loss, trauma, and resilience: Therapeutic work with ambiguous loss.* W. W. Norton.

81 *This is "social ambivalence."*

Montecinos (2020) calls for more study of how real-life social contexts might affect dissonance processes. I suggest that ambiguous loss is a prime example of a real-life social context that causes cognitive dissonance.

Montecinos, S. C. (2020). *New perspectives on cognitive dissonance theory* [Unpublished doctoral dissertation]. Stockholm University.

82 *Social psychologist Leon Festinger called this discomfort "cognitive dissonance."*

Ambivalence, then, from the social psychology perspective, remains closely connected to cognitive dissonance theory (Festinger, 1957), which says that when two beliefs are inconsistent, individuals experience negatively arousing cognitive conflict (called dissonance). Because the dissonance is aversive, the individuals try to reduce it by changing one belief or the other. See Sawacki et al. (2013) for more information.

Festinger, L. (1957). *A theory of cognitive dissonance.* Row, Peterson.

Sawacki, V., Wegener, D. T., Clark, J. K., Fabrigar, L. R., Smith, S. M., & Durso, G. R. (2013). Feeling conflicted and seeking information: When ambivalence enhances and diminishes selective exposure to attitude-consistent information. *Personality and Social Psychology Bulletin, 39*(6), 735–747. https://doi.org/10.1177/0146167213481388

85 *Left behind, we face the "savage pain."*

Ⅰ   The term "savage pain" is from *The Book of Job* (Mitchell, 1992, p. 21).

Mitchell, S. (1992). *The book of Job.* Harper Perennial.

85 *For this reason, I use the phrase "discover new hope."*

Ⅰ   Here, I must clear up a serious misunderstanding. Originally in 2006, I titled this guideline simply Discovering Hope (Boss, 2006). This title led to the unfortunate assumption that I was encouraging people to continue hoping for a missing person to return, that a missing soldier would come walking out of the jungle, that an ex-partner would return after a divorce, that a loved one with dementia would recover. That is not at all what I meant by my original title.

Boss, P. (2006). *Loss, trauma, and resilience: Therapeutic work with ambiguous loss.* W. W. Norton.

Chapter 8: If Not Closure, What's Normal Grief?

91 *I remember saying out loud to myself, "I'll never be happy again."*

Ⅰ   In 1952 alone, nearly 60,000 children were infected with the polio virus; thousands were paralyzed, and more than 3,000 died. Hospitals used iron lung machines to keep polio victims alive (Beaubien, 2012). In 1921, Franklin Delano Roosevelt contracted polio and was paralyzed for the rest of his life (https://www.fdrlibrary.org/polio). He became president of the United States in 1933 (https://www.fdrlibrary.org/fdr-presidency). For most of his presidency, he sat in a wheelchair, unable to walk. He started the March of Dimes to support scientists who were searching for a polio vaccine (https://www.fdrlibrary.org/polio). It was discovered and became available (Beaubien, 2012) just after my brother died.

Beaubien, J. (2012, October 15). *Wiping out polio: How the U.S. snuffed out a killer.* NPR. https://www.npr.org/sections/health-shots/2012/10/16/162670836/wiping-out-polio-how-the-u-s-snuffed-out-a-killer

92 *Unfortunately, today, that early focus on normal grief has been nearly lost in a sea of pathologies with an emphasis on grief as illness.*

The exclusion of normal grief in *DSM*-5 (American Psychiatric Association, 2013) is still being debated.

American Psychiatric Association. (2013). *Diagnostic and statistical manual of mental disorders* (5th ed.). https://doi.org/10.1176/appi.books.9780890425596

96 *I sensed they too were searching for meaning.*

Today, researchers agree that finding meaning is more helpful than seeking closure (Becvar, 2001; Bonanno, 2004, 2019; Boss, 1999, 2006, 2011; Harris, 2010; Kissane & Hooghe, 2011; Kissane & Parnes, 2014; Neimeyer et al., 2011; Roos, 2002; Walsh & McGoldrick, 2004).

Becvar, D. (2001). *In the presence of grief: Helping family members resolve death, dying, and bereavement issues.* Guilford Press.

Bonanno, G. A. (2004). Loss, trauma, and human resilience: Have we underestimated the human capacity to thrive after extremely aversive events? *American Psychologist,* 59(1), 20–28. https://doi.org/10.1037/0003-066x.59.1.20

Bonanno, G. A. (2019). *The other side of sadness: What the new science for bereavement tells us about life after loss.* Basic Books. (Original work published 2009)

Boss, P. (1999). *Ambiguous loss: Learning to live with unresolved grief.* Harvard University Press.

Boss, P. (2006). *Loss, trauma, and resilience: Therapeutic work with ambiguous loss.* W. W. Norton.

Boss, P. (2011). *Loving someone who has dementia: How to find hope while coping with stress and grief.* Jossey-Bass.

Harris, D. (Ed.). (2010). *Counting our losses: Reflecting on change, loss, and transition in everyday life.* Routledge. https://doi.org/10.4324/9780203860731

Kissane, D. W., & Hooghe, A. (2011). Family therapy for the bereaved. In R. A. Neimeyer, D. L. Harris, H. R. Winokuer, & G. F. Thornton (Eds.),

Grief and bereavement in contemporary society: Bridging research and practice (pp. 287–302). Routledge/Taylor & Francis.

Kissane, D. W., & Parnes. F. (Eds.). (2014). *Bereavement care for families*. Routledge. https://doi.org/10.4324/9780203084618

Neimeyer, R. A., Harris, D. L., Winokuer, H. R., & Thornton, G. F. (Eds.). (2011). *Grief and bereavement in contemporary society: Bridging research and practice*. Routledge/Taylor & Francis Group. https://doi.org/10.1080/01924788.2013.845721

Roos, S. (2002). *Chronic sorrow: A living loss*. Brunner-Routledge.

Walsh, F., & McGoldrick, M. (Eds.). (2004). *Living beyond loss: Death in the family* (2nd ed.). W. W. Norton.

98 *But to psychologists, mourning is a great riddle.*

From Freud's 1915 essay "On Transience" (Freud, 1957).

Freud, S. (1957). On transience. In J. Strachey (Ed. & Trans.), *The standard edition of the complete psychological works of Sigmund Freud: Vol. 14* (pp. 305-307). Hogarth Press. (Original work published 1915)

103 *I thought of a painting by the Swiss Italian painter Giovanni Segantini, titled* Vergehen, *which depicts a cloud above the house after a death, meaning the person had died and was passing* (vergehen) *overhead but still lingering.*

Displayed in the Segantini Museum in St. Moritz, Switzerland.

Chapter 9: Loss and Change

105 *I learned about the paradox of change from psychiatrist Carl Whitaker.*

Carl Whitaker was professor of psychiatry at UW–Madison, and I was a doctoral student allowed in his seminars because no women were in psychiatric residency at that time. Later, when I was a professor at the University of Minnesota, he came to St. Paul, Minnesota, on June 26, 1985, to speak at a family therapy conference on change. The quotes are from my notes taken during his presentation.

106 *The shift comes when we least expect it.*

Whitaker often told me that insight comes after experience, not before it. I agreed about the irresolvable dialectic but did not agree that it was so linear. Yes, the tension was irresolvable, but experience begets insight, and insight begets experience. It is circular.

107   *Pushing ahead during a deadly pandemic, for example, living life the way one always did, ignoring the danger, avoiding new information, was first-order change—and dangerous.*

For more on "information avoidance," see Golman et al. (2017).

Golman, R., Hagmann, D., & Loewenstein, G. (2017). Information avoidance. *Journal of Economic Literature*, 55(1), 96–135. https://doi.org/10.1257/jel.20151245

114   *Nearby there was and still is a Say Their Names Cemetery, where 100 Black Americans who died at the hands of law enforcement are each named on a headstone.*

The headstones include George Floyd, Breonna Taylor, Michael Brown, Emmett Till, Trayvon Martin, Philando Castile, and Eric Garner.

References

Epigraph

vii *"Like enduring a lesson that one is resisting, I learned with each loss that "getting over it" was not possible. I now walk with the tension of imperfect solutions and balance them with the joys and passions in my daily life. I intentionally hold the opposing ideas of absence and presence, because I have learned that most human relationships are indeed both."*

Adapted from Boss, P. (2006). *Loss, trauma, and resilience: Therapeutic work with ambiguous loss.* W. W. Norton; p. 210.

Preface

xvi *Research shows that we do better to live with grief than to deny it or close the door on it.*

Boss, P., & Carnes, D. (2012). The myth of closure. *Family Process, 51*(4), 456–469. https://doi.org/10.1111/famp.12005

Harris, D. (Ed.). (2010). *Counting our losses: Reflecting on change, loss, and transition in everyday life.* Routledge. https://doi.org/10.4324/9780203860731

Kissane, D. W., & Parnes, F. (Eds.). (2014). *Bereavement care for families.* Routledge. https://doi.org/10.4324/9780203084618

Klass, D., Silverman, P. R., & Nickman, S. (Eds.). (1996). *Continuing bonds: New understandings of grief.* Taylor & Francis.

Neimeyer, R. A., Harris, D. L., Winokuer, H. R., & Thornton, G. F. (Eds.). (2011). *Grief and bereavement in contemporary society: Bridging research and practice.* Routledge/Taylor & Francis Group. https://doi.org/10.1080/01924788.2013.845721

xvi   *As Anderson Cooper said, this time in a 60 Minutes interview with Joaquin Phoenix, discussing the actor's loss of his brother, River Phoenix, "There's no timeline for grief."*

60 Minutes. (2020, September 13). *Joaquin Phoenix: A three-decade career filled with dark, complicated characters. CBS News.* https://www.cbsnews.com/news/joker-joaquin-phoenix-grants-anderson-cooper-a-rare-interview-on-60-minutes-2020-01-12/

xvi   *I've watched late-night talk shows since Jack Paar and Dick Cavett were hosts and so was listening when Stephen Colbert was talking with then Vice President Joe Biden about loss.*

The Late Show with Stephen Colbert. (2017, November 13). *VP Joe Biden is finding a way through grief.* YouTube. https://www.youtube.com/watch?v=Gl_qYPWDWF8

xvii   *Clarifying that the quote originated with The Lord of the Rings author J. R. R. Tolkien, the two men continued their candid and heartfelt talk about both of their tragic losses years ago.*

Anderson Cooper 360. (2019, August 18). *Stephen Colbert and Anderson Cooper's beautiful conversation about grief.* YouTube. https://www.youtube.com/watch?v=YB46h1koicQ

Chapter 1: Ambiguous Loss

3   *Ambiguous losses then lead to a disenfranchised grief because others do not see the loss as credible and worthy of grief.*

Doka, K. (1989). *Disenfranchised grief: Recognizing hidden sorrow.* Lexington Books.

9   *About 40% of the families of those still missing from 9/11 have no proof of death and are left holding the ambiguity of loss.*

Alsharif, M. (2019, October 18). *New York 9/11 victim identified 18 years after attack.* CNN. https://www.cnn.com/2019/10/18/us/9-11-victim-identified-18-years-later/index.html

10   *In addition to these catastrophic events, there are also everyday examples of physical ambiguous loss—breakups, separations, divorce, migration and immigration—and the loss of job security of close to*

a million mothers who quit their paid employment to take care of their children once schools and day care centers closed due to the coronavirus.

Gogoi, P. (2020, October 28). *Stuck-at-home moms: The pandemic's devastating toll on women.* NPR. https://www.npr.org/2020/10/28/928253674/stuck-at-home-moms-the-pandemics-devastating-toll-on-women

Chapter 2: The Myth of Closure

19   *"Because in the end, I actually have NO control over other people's destinies, but I can continue to accept and grow in mine."*

Personal communication. Also see Johnson, S. M. (2015). *Life is beautiful: How a lost girl became a true, confident child of God.* Morgan James.

19   *She also wrote about closure and the hurt it causes: "People wanted to call me a 'widow' right after he disappeared. . . . They would say, 'Oh, Donna, just call yourself a widow. It will make your life easier and no one will know the difference . . .'"*

Boss, P., & Carnes, D. (2012). The myth of closure. *Family Process, 51*(4), 456–469. https://doi.org/10.1111/famp.12005; p. 457.

19   *"It was another way of tucking away what happened under the cultural veneer of a closure word."*

Boss, P., & Carnes, D. (2012). The myth of closure. *Family Process, 51*(4), 456–469. https://doi.org/10.1111/famp.12005; p. 457.

20   *"Alzheimer's is handled a bit easier, I think, because of its frequency now, but even so, there is a 'hush' in the room when it is discussed, as though if we talk in a hush about this loss of a living person, it might be less horrible. It might not happen to us."*

Boss, P., & Carnes, D. (2012). The myth of closure. *Family Process, 51*(4), 456–469. https://doi.org/10.1111/famp.12005; pp. 459–460.

20   *For Sarah, while referring to her father and brother as "a part of my soul that will remain for eternity," her story gradually changed over the years from one of immense trauma and loss to one of higher purpose—raising her own children now in a healthier environment than she experienced and honoring her deceased father, who always*

wanted her to go to college, by becoming a licensed family therapist who can help others.

Johnson, S. M. (2015). *Life is beautiful: How a lost girl became a true, confident child of God.* Morgan James; Dedication.

21   *They are both at peace with a "continuing bond."*

Klass, D., Silverman, P. R., & Nickman, S. (Eds.). (1996). *Continuing bonds: New understandings of grief.* Taylor & Francis.

21   *"People try to find closure by planting trees, acquiring memorial tattoos, forgiving murderers, watching killers die, talking to offenders, writing letters, burning letters, burning wedding dresses, burying wedding rings, casting spells, taking trips to Hawaii, buying expensive pet urns, committing suicide, talking to dead people, reviewing autopsies, and planning funerals."*

Berns, N. (2011). *Closure: The rush to end grief and what it costs us.* Temple University Press. https://doi.org/10.1093/sf/sos124; p. 2.

22   *As referred to earlier, Mitch Albom wrote, "Death ends a life, not a relationship."*

Albom, M. (2017). *Tuesdays with Morrie.* Broadway Books; p. 174.

23   *Berns said that after giving birth to her stillborn son, people encouraged her to move on from her grief—or assumed she had already done so.*

Berns, N. (2011). *Closure: The rush to end grief and what it costs us.* Temple University Press. https://doi.org/10.1093/sf/sos124

23   *This is when she first became wary of the term and also of businesses and politicians who use closure to sell products and agendas.*

Berns, N. (2011). *Closure: The rush to end grief and what it costs us.* Temple University Press. https://doi.org/10.1093/sf/sos124

24   *Millions have been sickened by or died from the coronavirus.*

Coronavirus Resource Center. (n.d.). Johns Hopkins University & Medicine. *Home page.* Retrieved July 15, 2021, from https://coronavirus.jhu.edu/.

Chapter 3: Racism as Unresolved Loss

28   *But there is another tool that family therapists use—family of origin work.*

McGoldrick, M., & Gerson, R. (1985). *Genograms in family assessment.* W. W. Norton.

McGoldrick, M., Gerson, R., & Petry, S. (2020). *Genograms: Assessment and treatment* (4th ed.). W. W. Norton.

McGoldrick, M., Gerson, R., & Shellenberger, S. (1999). *Genograms: Assessment and intervention* (2nd ed.). W. W. Norton.

28 *Based on our history of the dead and missing from the Civil War, genocide, and slavery of people of color, we are indeed a "republic of suffering."*

Faust, D. G. (2009). *The republic of suffering: Death and the American Civil War.* Vintage Books.

28 *We are a nation born out of ambiguous losses still carrying the anger and grief that lingers. It is now time for a reckoning.*

Boss, P. (2019). Building resilience: The example of ambiguous loss. In B. Huppertz (Ed.), *Approaches to psychic trauma: Theory and practice* (pp. 91–105). Rowman & Littlefield.

Boss, P., & Ishii, C. (2015). Trauma and ambiguous loss: The lingering presence of the physically absent. In K. E. Cherry (Ed.), *Traumatic stress and long-term recovery* (pp. 271–289). Springer International. https://doi.org/10.1007/978-3-319-18866-9

DeGruy, J. (2017). *Post traumatic slave syndrome: America's legacy of enduring injury and healing* (Rev. ed.). Joy DeGruy.

31 *"Consequently, I despair in finding language to express adequately the deep feeling of my soul, as I contemplate the past history of my life."*

Bibb, H. (1849). *Narrative of the life and adventures of Henry Bibb, an American slave, written by himself.* https://docsouth.unc.edu/neh/bibb/bibb.html; pp. 14–15.

31 *Is this a biological process?*

Goosby, B. J., & Heidbrink, C. (2013). The transgenerational consequences of discrimination on African-American health outcomes. *Sociology Compass, 7*(8), 630–643. https://doi.org/10.1111/soc4.12054

Powledge, T. M. (2011). Behavioral epigenetics: How nurture shapes nature. *BioScience, 61*(8), 588–592. https://doi.org/10.1525/bio.2011.61.8.4

31 *Or is it a social process?*

DeGruy, J. (2017). *Post traumatic slave syndrome: America's legacy of enduring injury and healing* (Rev. ed.). Joy DeGruy.

Pinderhughes, E. (2004). The multigenerational transmission of loss and trauma: The African-American experience. In F. Walsh & M. McGoldrick (Eds.), *Living beyond loss: Death in the family* (2nd ed., pp. 161–181). W. W. Norton.

31 *On the biological side, inheritance of the effects of trauma is of key interest in epigenetics, the study of inheritable changes in DNA that change its expression, but not the gene itself.*

Goosby, B. J., & Heidbrink, C. (2013). The transgenerational consequences of discrimination on African-American health outcomes. *Sociology Compass, 7*(8), 630–643. https://doi.org/10.1111/soc4.12054

Powledge, T. M. (2011). Behavioral epigenetics: How nurture shapes nature. *BioScience, 61*(8), 588–592. https://doi.org/10.1525/bio.2011.61.8.4

31 *We know from past studies of Holocaust mothers and their children that the effects of trauma can be passed down from mother to child.*

Dashorst, P., Mooren, T. M., Kleber, R. J., de Jong, P. J., & Huntjens, R. J. (2019). Intergenerational consequences of the Holocaust on offspring mental health: A systematic review of associated factors and mechanisms. *European Journal of Psychotraumatology, 10*(1), 1654065. https://doi.org/10.1080/20008198.2019.1654065

31 *Clinician and researcher Bessel van der Kolk also finds that past trauma affects our bodies.*

van der Kolk, B. A. (2014). *The body keeps the score: Brain, mind, and body in the healing of trauma.* Viking. https://doi.org/10.1080/0092623X.2017.1348102

32 *Meanwhile, from a more social-psychological perspective, Joy DeGruy proposes a theory of post-traumatic slave syndrome.*

DeGruy, J. (2017). *Post traumatic slave syndrome: America's legacy of enduring injury and healing* (Rev. ed.). Joy DeGruy.

33 *"I made a regular business of it, and never gave it up, until I had broken the bands of slavery, and landed myself safely in Canada, where I was regarded as a man, and not as a thing."*

Bibb, H. (1849). *Narrative of the life and adventures of Henry Bibb, an American slave, written by himself.* https://docsouth.unc.edu/neh/bibb/bibb.html; pp. 15–16.

34 *The policeman's knee had been on his neck for over nine minutes.*

Boone, A. (2020, June 3). One week in Minneapolis. *Star Tribune.* https://www.startribune.com/george-floyd-death-ignited-pro tests-far-beyond-minneapolis-police-minnesota/569930771/

Forliti, A. (2021, March 4). Prosecutors: Officer was on Floyd's neck for about 9 minutes. *AP News.* https://apnews.com/article/ trials-derek-chauvin-minneapolis-racial-injustice-060f6e9e8b7079 505a1b096a68311c2b

34 *My colleague in family therapy, Elaine Pinderhughes, was one of the first to teach me that historical context matters for human development and that being traumatized instead of nurtured will affect not only children but their offspring as well.*

Pinderhughes, E. (2004). The multigenerational transmission of loss and trauma: The African American experience. In F. Walsh & M. McGoldrick (Eds.), *Living beyond loss: Death in the family* (2nd ed., pp. 161–181). W. W. Norton.

35 *As a family therapist, she wrote that "as a consequence of their 400-year-old entrapment in racism," their losses were "nothing short of cataclysmic."*

Pinderhughes, E. (2004). The multigenerational transmission of loss and trauma: The African American experience. In F. Walsh & M. McGoldrick (Eds.), *Living beyond loss: Death in the family* (2nd ed., pp. 161-181). W. W. Norton.

35 *Overall, the context in which early African Americans were forced to live has affected future generations.*

Pinderhughes, E. (2004). The multigenerational transmission of loss and trauma: The African American experience. In F. Walsh & M. McGoldrick (Eds.), *Living beyond loss: Death in the family* (2nd ed., pp. 161–181). W. W. Norton; p. 161.

35 *There were the shameful events of the Reconstruction Period, family losses due to Northern migration, and the deindustrialization due to technology.*

Staples, R. (1988). An overview of race and marital status. In H. P. McAdoo (Ed.), *Black families* (pp. 187–189). Sage. https:// doi.org/10.4135/9781452226026.n19

35 *During the 1960s to the 1980s, blue-collar jobs were stable in the factories of the North, but racial inequities still existed and these factory*

jobs eventually gave way to technology, which broke up many Black families.

Gould, E. (2018, December 19). *The impact of manufacturing employment decline on Black and white Americans.* VOXeu/CEPR. https://voxeu.org/article/manufacturing-decline-has-hurt-black-americans-more

36 *"This means that white America must give up the benefits of racism."*

Pinderhughes, E. (2004). The multigenerational transmission of loss and trauma: The African American experience. In F. Walsh & M. McGoldrick (Eds.), *Living beyond loss: Death in the family* (2nd ed., pp. 161–181). W. W. Norton; p. 179.

Chapter 4: Resilience: Our Best Hope in the Face of Ambiguous Loss

39 *The surprise of resilience is that this ancient bonsai tree survived the atomic bomb blast in Hiroshima during World War II.*

Siddiqui, F. (2015, August 2). This 390-year-old bonsai tree survived an atomic bomb, and no one knew until 2001. *Washington Post.* https://www.washingtonpost.com/local/the-390-year-old-tree-that-survived-an-atomic-bomb/2015/08/02/3f824dae-3945-11e5-8e98-115a3cf7d7ae_story.html

40 *The assumption is that we learn something from the stress we experience and thus become stronger for it.*

Boss, P., Bryant, C., & Mancini, J. (2017). *Family stress management: A contextual approach* (3rd ed.). Sage. https://doi.org/10.4135/9781506352206.

40 *Social worker Hollingsworth writes that "when resilience is defined as being confronted with adversity and surviving and prospering in spite of it, there certainly is evidence of it in Black families."*

Hollingsworth, L. D. (2013). Resilience in Black families. In D. Becvar (Ed.), *Handbook of family resilience* (pp. 229–244). Springer. https://doi.org/10.1007/978-1-4614-3917-2_14; p. 240.

41 *That is, while the first studies on resilience were done with poor and homeless children in Hawaii, the problems of homelessness and poverty are avoidable. They can be ameliorated.*

Werner, E. E., Bierman, J. M., & French, F. E. (1971). *The chil-*

dren of Kauai: A longitudinal study from the prenatal period to age ten. University of Hawaii Press.

Garmezy, N. (1983). Stressors of childhood. In N. Garmezy & M. Rutter (Eds.), *Stress, coping, and development in children* (pp. 43–84). McGraw-Hill.

41 *Family and community can both be sources of resilience—and barriers to it.*

Boss, P. (2006). *Loss, trauma, and resilience: Therapeutic work with ambiguous loss.* W. W. Norton.

Boss, P. (2013). Resilience as tolerance for ambiguity. In D. S. Becvar (Ed.), *Handbook of family resilience* (pp. 285–297). Springer. https://doi.org/10.1007/978-1-4614-3917-2_17

Boss, P., Beaulieu, L., Wieling, E., Turner, W., & LaCruz, S. (2003). Healing loss, ambiguity, and trauma: A community-based intervention with families of union workers missing after the 9/11 attack in New York City. *Journal of Marital and Family Therapy, 29*(4), 455–467. https://doi.org/10.1111/j.1752-0606.2003.tb01688.x

Landau, J., & Saul, J. (2004). Facilitating family and community resilience in response to major disaster. In F. Walsh & M. McGoldrick (Eds.), *Living beyond loss: Death in the family* (pp. 285–309). W. W. Norton.

Robins, S. (2010). Ambiguous loss in a non-Western context: Families of the disappeared in postconflict Nepal. *Family Relations, 59*(3), 253–268. https://doi.org/10.1111/j.1741-3729.2010.00600.x

42 *Resilience is more common than we think.*

Boss, P. (2006). *Loss, trauma, and resilience: Therapeutic work with ambiguous loss.* W. W. Norton.

Boss, P. (2013). Resilience as tolerance for ambiguity. In D. S. Becvar (Ed.), *Handbook of family resilience* (pp. 285–297). Springer. https://doi.org/10.1007/978-1-4614-3917-2_17

42 *Most people have a self-righting ability to cope.*

Bonanno, G. A. (2004). Loss, trauma, and human resilience: Have we underestimated the human capacity to thrive after extremely aversive events? *American Psychologist, 59*(1), 20–28. https://doi.org/10.1037/0003-066x.59.1.20

Bonanno, G. A. (2019). *The other side of sadness: What the new science of bereavement tells us about life after loss.* Basic Books. (Original work published 2009)

42   *There are multiple and unexpected pathways to resilience.*

Boss, P. (2006). *Loss, trauma, and resilience: Therapeutic work with ambiguous loss.* W. W. Norton.

Boss, P. (2013). Resilience as tolerance for ambiguity. In D. S. Becvar (Ed.), *Handbook of family resilience* (pp. 285–297). Springer. https://doi.org/10.1007/978-1-4614-3917-2_17

Bonanno, G. A., Field, N. P., Kovacevic, A., & Kaltman, S. (2002). Self-enhancement as a buffer against extreme adversity: Civil war in Bosnia and traumatic loss in the United States. *Personality and Social Psychology Bulletin, 28*(2), 184–196. https://doi.org/10.1177/0146167202282005

Bonanno, G. A., Noll, J. G., Putnam, F. W., O'Neill, M., & Trickett, P. K. (2003). Predicting the willingness to disclose childhood sexual abuse from measures of repressive coping and dissociative tendencies. *Child Maltreatment, 8*(4), 302–318. https://doi.org/10.1177/1077559503257066

Kobasa, S. C., Maddi, S. R., & Kahn, S. (1982). Hardiness and health: A prospective study. *Journal of Personality and Social Psychology, 42*(1), 168–177. https://doi.org/10.1037/0022-3514.42.1.168

43   *For children, resilience is often called "ordinary magic," meaning that kids are naturally flexible, and thus good adapters to situations of stress, even those with "substantial challenges."*

Masten, A. S. (2001). Ordinary magic: Resilience processes in development. *American Psychologist, 56*(3), 227–238. https://doi.org/10.1037/0003-066x.56.3.227

Masten, A. S. (2014). *Ordinary magic: Resilience in development.* Guilford Press.

Masten, A. S., & Coatsworth, J. D. (1998). The development of competence in favorable and unfavorable environments: Lessons from research on successful children. *American Psychologist, 53*(2), 205–220. https://doi.org/10.1037/0003-066x.53.2.205

43   *A "dandelion child" has the capacity to survive and even thrive in harsh circumstances, whereas an "orchid child" requires more nurturance to flourish.*

Ellis, B. J., & Boyce, W. T. (2008). Biological sensitivity to context. *Current Directions in Psychological Science, 17*(3), 183–187. https://doi.org/10.1111/j.1467-8721.2008.00571.x

43 *The point is that we can increase our resilience for managing stress by grappling with the problems of everyday life.*

Boss, P., Bryant, C., & Mancini, J. (2017). *Family stress management: A contextual approach* (3rd ed.). Sage. https://doi.org/10.4135/9781506352206

44 *"It was a selfless act," she said, "and it meant we were not alone. It gave us the tremendous support we were craving."*

Free, C. (2020, November 19). Utah hospital workers rushed to NYC to help with covid in the spring. NYC workers just returned the favor. *Washington Post*. https://www.washingtonpost.com/lifestyle/2020/11/19/utah-nyc-healthcare-covid-nurse/

45 *A psychological family is the family in one's heart and mind. It refers to our personal beliefs about who is in or out of our family.*

Boss, P. (2006). *Loss, trauma, and resilience: Therapeutic work with ambiguous loss.* W. W. Norton.

45 *Some form of the psychological family exists in all cultures, but in different ways.*

Boss, P. (2019). Building resilience: The example of ambiguous loss. In B. Huppertz (Ed.), *Approaches to psychic trauma: Theory and practice* (pp. 91–105). Rowman & Littlefield.

45 *During slavery, when parents were sold away, their children left behind were cared for by others in the community, a functional adaptation that we still see today.*

Bryant, C. M. (2018, Spring). African American fictive kin: Historical and contemporary notions. *Family Focus*, F10–F11. https://www.ncfr.org/ncfr-report/focus/fictive-kin

46 *Today, we also see psychological bonding in chosen family networks, for example, military families, expat families living in foreign countries, and kinship family networks among gender and sexual minorities.*

Catalpa, J., & Routon, J. M. (2018, Spring). Queer kinship: Family networks among sexual and gender minorities. *Family Focus*, F8–F9. https://www.ncfr.org/news/research-lgbtq-families-available-ncfr-members

46 *For example, after the 2011 tsunami in northeastern Japan, many survivors were comforted by knowing that their ancestors were now looking after loved ones who were washed away.*

Boss, P., & Ishii, C. (2015). Trauma and ambiguous loss: The lingering presence of the physically absent. In K. E. Cherry (Ed.), *Traumatic stress and long-term recovery* (pp. 271–289). Springer International. https://doi.org/10.1007/978-3-319-18866-9

Chapter 5: The Paradox of Absence and Presence

49 *There is no certainty that the lost person is dead or alive, if they will return, or where they, or their remains, might be.*

Boss, P. (1999). *Ambiguous loss: Learning to live with unresolved grief.* Harvard University Press.

Boss, P. (2004). Ambiguous loss. In F. Walsh & M. McGoldrick (Eds.), *Living beyond loss: Death in the family* (2nd ed., pp. 237–246). W. W. Norton.

49 *Yet, instead of these absolute reactions, many people learn to tolerate the ambiguity and live well despite it.*

Boss, P. (1999). *Ambiguous loss: Learning to live with unresolved grief.* Harvard University Press.

Boss, P. (2002). Ambiguous loss in families of the missing. *The Lancet, 360,* 39–40.

Boss, P. (2006). *Loss, trauma, and resilience: Therapeutic work with ambiguous loss.* W. W. Norton.

Boss, P., Beaulieu, L., Wieling, E., Turner, W., & LaCruz, S. (2003). Healing loss, ambiguity, and trauma: A community-based intervention with families of union workers missing after the 9/11 attack in New York City. *Journal of Marital and Family Therapy, 29*(4), 455–467. https://doi.org/10.1111/j.1752-0606.2003.tb01688.x

ICRC. (2013). *Accompanying the families of missing persons.* International Committee of the Red Cross. https://www.icrc.org/en/publication/4110-accompanying-families-missing-persons-practical-handbook

55 *As a result, they are abandoned on the shore and must roam the earth until there is certainty about their death.*

Butterworth, J. (2017). *The ferryman.* Nick Hern Books.

55 *For the Carney family in this play, the question is similar: how can the family members reach closure when there is no body to grieve?*
Boss, P. (2017). Ambiguous loss. *The ferryman* [playbill].

65 *Instead of absolute thinking, we shift to both/and thinking. This is resilience—being open to change; being able to hold two opposing ideas in your mind at the same time, as F. Scott Fitzgerald wrote.*
Fitzgerald, S. (1945). *The crack-up.* The New Directions.

Chapter 6: Both/And Thinking

60 *When we think about the loss of a family member or friend as both/and, we may be reminded of dialectical thinking, which means holding both a thesis and antithesis but eventually reaching a synthesis or blending of those two opposing facts.*
Meacham, J. (1999). Riegel, dialectics, and multiculturalism. *Human Development, 42*(3), 134–144. https://doi.org/10.1159/000022619

62 *As absurdity and rationality were at odds, our stress levels rose to crisis levels and immobilized us.*
Boss, P., Bryant, C., & Mancini, J. (2017). *Family stress management: A contextual approach* (3rd ed.). Sage. https://doi.org/10.4135/9781506352206

63 *Medical sociologist and stress expert Aaron Antonovsky said that if we think something is understandable, manageable, and meaningful, the stress it causes is less debilitating to one's health.*
Antonovsky, A. (1979). *Health, stress, and coping: New perspectives on mental and physical well-being.* Jossey-Bass.
Antonovsky, A. (1987). *Unraveling the mystery of health: How people manage stress and stay well.* Jossey-Bass.

Chapter 7: Six Guidelines for the Resilience to Live With Loss

70 *In no particular order, as indicated by the various connecting lines in Figure 7.1, the following guidelines can help build your resilience: finding meaning, adjusting need for mastery, reconstructing identity, normalizing ambivalence, revising attachment, and discovering new hope.*

Boss, P. (2006). *Loss, trauma, and resilience: Therapeutic work with ambiguous loss.* W. W. Norton.

73   *What psychologists tell us is that for most people, life is "pretty meaningful," even for those who have faced hard times.*

Heintzelman, S. J., & King, L. A. (2014). Life is pretty meaningful. *American Psychologist, 69*(6), 561–574. https://doi.org/10.1037/a0035049; p. 561.

73   *Viktor Frankl found meaning in a concentration camp; Antonovksy found it in hospitals working with cancer patients.*

Antonovsky, A. (1979). *Health, stress, and coping: New perspectives on mental and physical well-being.* Jossey-Bass.

Antonovsky, A. (1987). *Unraveling the mystery of health: How people manage stress and stay well.* Jossey-Bass.

Frankl, V. (2006). *Man's search for meaning.* Beacon Press. (Original English publication, 1959)

74   *We grieve individually and we grieve as a nation because, as President Biden said on the eve of his inauguration in a ceremony honoring those who died in the pandemic, "It's hard sometimes to remember. But that's how we heal. It's important to do that as a nation."*

Baker, P. (2021, January 19). On night before inauguration, Biden leads mourning for virus victims. *The New York Times.* https://www.nytimes.com/2021/01/19/us/politics/biden-inauguration-coronavirus.html

74   *I think of the Serenity Prayer: "God, give us grace to accept with serenity the things that cannot be changed, courage to change things that should be changed, and the wisdom to distinguish the one from the other."*

Sifton, E. (2003). *The Serenity Prayer: Faith and politics in times of peace and war.* W. W. Norton.; p. 7.

74   *Mastery is the ability to master challenges and have control over our lives.*

Pearlin, L. I., & Schooler, C. (1978). The structure of coping. *Journal of Health and Social Behavior, 19*(1), 2–21. https://doi.org/10.2307/2136319

75   *Being able to manage and solve problems is consistently shown to ease stress and trauma.*

Antonovsky, A. (1979). *Health, stress, and coping: New perspectives on mental and physical well-being.* Jossey-Bass.

Antonovsky, A. (1987). *Unraveling the mystery of health: How people manage stress and stay well.* Jossey-Bass.

Boss, P. (2013). Resilience as tolerance for ambiguity. In D. S. Becvar (Ed.), *Handbook of family resilience* (pp. 285–297). Springer. https://doi.org/10.1007/978-1-4614-3917-2_17

Boss, P. (2017). Families of the missing: Psychosocial effects and therapeutic approaches. *International Review of the Red Cross, 99*(2), 519–534. https://doi.org/10.1017/s1816383118000140

75 *When her husband died suddenly at the dinner table, she wrote, "This was one of those events. You sit down to dinner and life as you know it ends."*

Didion, J. (2005). *The year of magical thinking.* Vintage Books.; p. 98.

76 *Some time ago, I heard from a friend whose son went missing in the mountains of Idaho, and later was found dead.*

Francis, D. (2010). *Bringing Jon home: The wilderness search for Jon Francis.* Beaver's Pond Press.

76 *I told him that as a military officer, he was expected to master and control the most difficult situations, but the loss of his son was different.*

D. Francis, personal communications, June 30–July 1, 2018.

77 *Space engineers have taken a sample of rocks from the asteroid Bennu—so far away that it will take three years for the rocks to get back to earth for testing.*

NASA. (2020, October 20). *NASA's OSIRIS-REx spacecraft successfully touches asteroid.* National Aeronautics and Space Administration. https://www.nasa.gov/press-release/nasa-s-osiris-rex-spacecraft-successfully-touches-asteroid

77 *Mastering and controlling disease is not as clear. Thus far, only one disease—small pox—has been eradicated worldwide. Polio is nearly eliminated but still occurs where vaccines are mistrusted.*

The History of Vaccines (n.d.). *Disease eradication.* https://ftp.historyofvaccines.org/multilanguage/content/articles/disease-eradication

79 *Others serve as a mirror as you discover who you are now.*

Boss, P. (2006). *Loss, trauma, and resilience: Therapeutic work with ambiguous loss.* W. W. Norton.

81 *Ambivalence is the child of ambiguity.*

Dahl, C. M., & Boss, P. (2020). Ambiguous loss: Theory-based guidelines for therapy with individuals, families, and communities. In K. S. Wampler, M. Rastogi, & R. Singh (Eds.), *The handbook of systemic family therapy: Vol. 4. Systemic family therapy and global health issues* (pp. 127–151). Wiley. https://doi.org/10.1002/9781119788409.ch6

80 *The poet Sharon Olds wrote about her dying father: "I wanted to watch my father die because I hated him. Oh, I loved him."*

Olds, S. (1992). *The father.* Knopf.; p. 71.

81 *"In that moment I hated her and her power absolutely. In that moment I loved her and her power absolutely."*

Sexton, L. G. (1994). *Searching for Mercy Street: My journey back to my mother, Anne Sexton.* Little, Brown.; p. 161.

81 *This is "social ambivalence."*

Merton, R. K., & Barber, E. (1963). Sociological ambivalence. In E. Tiryakian (Ed.), *Sociological theory, values, and sociocultural change* (pp. 91–120). Free Press. https://doi.org/10.4324/9781315129976-5

81 *This social-psychological view of ambivalence externalizes the cause and creates less resistance in acknowledging our mixed emotions.*

Merton, R. K., & Barber, E. (1963). Sociological ambivalence. In E. Tiryakian (Ed.), *Sociological theory, values, and sociocultural change* (pp. 91–120). Free Press. https://doi.org/10.4324/9781315129976-5

82 *Social psychologist Leon Festinger called this discomfort "cognitive dissonance."*

Festinger, L. (1957). *A theory of cognitive dissonance.* Row, Peterson.

83 *Psychologist John Bowlby, founder of attachment theory, wrote this about widows and widowers and the value of continuing bonds: "It is precisely because they are willing for their feelings of attachment to the dead spouse to persist that their sense of identity is preserved*

and they become able to reorganize their lives along lines they find meaningful."

Bowlby, J. (1980). *Loss, sadness, and depression.* Basic Books; p. 98.

87 *Finally, we need to be aware that profound loss can still occur even after a missing person is found. I think of the Tom Hanks film,* Cast Away, *and numerous real life cases—the few 9/11 missing found alive, and the many missing-in-action from all wars found either alive or dead—like Francine du Plessix Gray's pilot father who went missing during World War II. Years later, she found him buried in a grave in France.*

du Plessix Gray, F. (2000). At large and small: The work of mourning. *American Scholar, 69*(3), 7–13.

Zemeckis, R. (Director, Producer). (2000). *Cast away* [Film]. ImageMovers, Playtone.

88 *Change happens even when hopes come true. When a missing person is found or when girls kidnapped by terrorists return home and are stigmatized by their families or village, the reversal of loss is also painful—and requires change.*

Associated Press. (2019, October 14). Jayme Closs "reclaiming her life" as she marks first anniversary of abduction. *The Guardian.* https://www.theguardian.com/us-news/2019/oct/14/jayme-closs-abduction-wisconsin-first-anniversary-statement

Searcy, D. (2016, May 18). Victims of Boko Haram, and now shunned by their communities. *New York Times.* https://www.nytimes.com/2016/05/19/world/africa/boko-haram-victims-nigeria.html

88 *Paraphrasing Viktor Frankl, there is no meaning without hope and no hope without meaning.*

Frankl, V. (2006). *Man's search for meaning.* Beacon Press. (Original English publication, 1959)

Chapter 8: If Not Closure, What's Normal Grief?

89 *So far, I have not written much about grief, as this book is mostly about loss and its nuances. But it's time now. In 2020, headlines read: "Virus Crisis Explodes; 'Desperate' Situation."*

Snowbeck, C. (2020, November 15). Virus crisis explodes. *Star Tribune,* A1.

89 *Deaths Climb Fast . . . ; "Horrifying" Toll.*

Mervosh, S., Goodman, J. D., & Bosman, J. (2020, November 15). "Horrifying" toll seen in coming months. *New York Times*, p. 1.

89 *Worldwide, over 4 million people have died from COVID-19 and its mutations.*

Coronavirus Resource Center. (n.d.). Johns Hopkins University & Medicine. *Home page.* Retrieved August 10, 2021, from https://coronavirus.jhu.edu/

93 *Normal grief is the natural and expected response of deep sorrow and pain after losing someone or something you love.*

Boss, P. (2011). *Loving someone who has dementia: How to find hope while coping with stress and grief.* Jossey-Bass.

93 *With normal grief, many of the signs are similar to those of a major depression—feelings of emptiness, fatigue, perhaps loss of appetite, inability to sleep, inability to feel pleasure, and sometimes guilt—but there are two essential signs that your grief is normal. First, such symptoms become less intense over weeks and months, and second, you do not have feelings of worthlessness and self-loathing. (For precise information, see American Psychiatric Association, 2013, reference.)*

American Psychiatric Association. (2013). *Diagnostic and statistical manual of mental disorders* (5th ed.). https://doi.org/10.1176/appi.books.9780890425596

93 *The sadness of loss comes and goes in something like waves, what researchers call "oscillations."*

Bonanno, G. A. (2019). *The other side of sadness: What the new science of bereavement tells us about life after loss.* Basic Books. (Original work published 2009)

93 *We can experience some pleasure again.*

Boss, P., & Dahl, C. M. (2014). Family therapy for the unresolved grief of ambiguous loss. In D. W. Kissane & F. Parnes (Eds.), *Bereavement care for families* (pp. 171–182). Routledge.

94 *Also seek professional help if after several months or a year, your grief remains so intense that it still impairs your daily functioning.*

Mayo Clinic. (n.d.). *Complicated grief.* https://www.mayoclinic.org/diseases-conditions/complicated-grief/symptoms-causes/syc-20360374

96 *In 1996, a major challenge came in a book called* Continuing Bonds. *It was compiled by Klass and colleagues who proposed that after death, bonds continued.*

Klass, D., Silverman, P. R., & Nickman, S. (Eds.). (1996). *Continuing bonds: New understandings of grief.* Taylor & Francis.

96 *When a patient expressed her condolences to Freud about Sophie's untimely death (she was only 27), he responded by pulling a locket on a chain from his vest pocket, patted it, and said, "She is here."*

Gay, P. (2006). *Freud: A life for our time.* W. W. Norton.

97 *"Although we know after such a loss the acute state of mourning will subside, we also know we shall remain inconsolable and will never find a substitute. No matter what may fill the gap, even if it be filled completely, it nevertheless remains something else. And this is how it should be, it is the only way of perpetuating that love which we do not want to relinquish."*

Freud, S. (1960). Letter to Binswanger (letter 239). In E. L. Freud (Ed.), *Letters of Sigmund Freud.* Basic Books.

97 *After years of suffering from mouth cancer and knowing his time was now limited, Freud wrote to his good friend, Marie Bonaparte:* . . . *"I hope you will soon console yourself over my death and let me go on living in your friendly recollections—the only kind of limited immortality I recognize."*

von Unwerth, M. (2006). *Freud's requiem.* Riverhead Books.; p. 170.

97 *Back then, Freud's ideas were more erudite, but the lines I value are these: "Mourning over the loss of something that we have loved or admired seems so natural to the layman that he regards it as self-evident. But to psychologists, mourning is a great riddle."*

von Unwerth, M. (2006). *Freud's requiem.* Riverhead Books.; p. 217.

98 *After a series of debilitating strokes, and shortly before she died, Kübler-Ross called her own process of dying a nightmare.*

Kübler-Ross, E., & Kessler, D. (2005). *On grief and grieving: Finding the meaning of grief through the five stages of loss.* Scribner.; p. 216.

98 *She acknowledged the changing face of grief today and regretted that her ideas were so misunderstood.*

Kübler-Ross, E., & Kessler, D. (2000). *Life lessons: Two experts on death and dying teach us about the mysteries of life and living.* Scribner.

Kübler-Ross, E., & Kessler, D. (2005). *On grief and grieving: Finding the meaning of grief through the five stages of loss.* Scribner.

98   *When asked how long it took to get through the five stages, she wrote, "Grief is not just a series of events, stages, or timelines. Our society places enormous pressure on us to get over loss, to get through the grief."*

Kübler-Ross, E., & Kessler, D. (2005). *On grief and grieving: Finding the meaning of grief through the five stages of loss.* Scribner.; p. 203.

98   *Up to her last days, Elisabeth Kübler-Ross continued to correct the misuse of her five stages: "They were never meant to help tuck messy emotions into neat packages. The five stages—denial, anger, bargaining, depression, and acceptance—are part of the framework that makes up our learning to live with the one we lost. . . But they are not stops on some linear timeline in grief."*

Kübler-Ross, E., & Kessler, D. (2005). *On grief and grieving: Finding the meaning of grief through the five stages of loss.* Scribner.; p. 7.

99   *Just before her death, she wrote, "Acceptance is a process that we experience, not a final stage with an end point."*

Kübler-Ross, E., & Kessler, D. (2005). *On grief and grieving: Finding the meaning of grief through the five stages of loss.* Scribner.; p. 27.

99   *"Being ill for nine years has forced me to learn patience. . . . I know death is close, but not quite yet. I lie here like so many people over the years, in a bed surrounded by flowers and looking out a big window. A room not much different from that first good death I saw. These last years have been like being stuck on a runway, not allowed to die and leave this earth, but not allowed to go back to the gate and fully live."*

Kübler-Ross, E., & Kessler, D. (2005). *On grief and grieving: Finding the meaning of grief through the five stages of loss.* Scribner.; p. 215.

99   *"The process of dying when it is prolonged like mine is a nightmare. I have struggled with the constant pain and paralysis. After many*

years of total independence, it is a difficult state of being. It has been a long nine years since my stroke, and I am anxious to die—graduate as I call it. I now know that the purpose of my life is more than these stages. . . . It is not just about knowing the stages. It is not just about the life lost but also the life lived. . . . I am so much more than five stages. And so are you."

Kübler-Ross, E., & Kessler, D. (2005). *On grief and grieving: Finding the meaning of grief through the five stages of loss.* Scribner.; p. 216.

100 *An Austrian psychiatrist and concentration camp survivor from the World War II Holocaust, his ideas about the ongoing presence of lost loved ones, as opposed to closure, moved me.*

Frankl, V. (2006). *Man's search for meaning.* Beacon Press. (Original English publication, 1959)

100 *Early on, his focus on the search for meaning made sense to me and is now supported by research affirming that we can live with loss if we find some meaning in it.*

Becvar, D. (2001). *In the presence of grief: Helping family members resolve death, dying, and bereavement issues.* Guilford Press.

Bonanno, G. A. (2004). Loss, trauma, and human resilience: Have we underestimated the human capacity to thrive after extremely aversive events? *American Psychologist, 59*(1), 20–28. https://doi.org/10.1037/0003-066x.59.1.20

Bonanno, G. A. (2019). *The other side of sadness: What the new science of bereavement tells us about life after loss.* Basic Books. (Original work published 2009)

Kissane, D. W., & Hooghe, A. (2011). Family therapy for the bereaved. In R. A. Neimeyer, D. L. Harris, H. R. Winokuer, & G. F. Thornton (Eds.), *Grief and bereavement in contemporary society: Bridging research and practice* (pp. 287–302). Routledge/Taylor & Francis.

Neimeyer, R. A., Harris, D. L., Winokuer, H. R., & Thornton, G. F. (Eds.). (2011). *Grief and bereavement in contemporary society: Bridging research and practice.* Routledge/Taylor & Francis. https://doi.org/10.1080/01924788.2013.845721

100 *"My mind still clung to the image of my wife. A thought crossed my mind: I didn't even know if she were still alive. I knew only one*

thing—which I have learned well by now: Love goes very far beyond the physical person of the beloved. It finds its deepest meaning in [their] spiritual being, [their] inner self. Whether or not [she] is actually present, whether or not [she] is still alive at all, ceases somehow to be of importance."

Frankl, V. (2006). *Man's search for meaning.* Beacon Press. (Original English publication, 1959); p. 38.

101   *"My mind clung to my wife's image, imagining it with an uncanny acuteness. I heard her answering me, saw her smile, her frank and encouraging look. Real or not, her look was then more luminous than the sun, which was beginning to rise. A thought transfixed me: for the first time in my life I saw the truth, as it is set into song by so many poets, proclaimed as the final wisdom by so many thinkers. The truth—that love is the ultimate and the highest goal to which [people] can aspire. Then I grasped the meaning of the greatest secret that human poetry and human thought and belief have to impart: The salvation of [human beings] is through love and in love. I understood how a [person] who has nothing left in this world still may know bliss, be it only for a brief moment, in the contemplation of [one's] beloved."*

Frankl, V. (2006). *Man's search for meaning.* Beacon Press. (Original English publication, 1959); p. 37.

103   *Caregivers know about "chronic sorrow."*

Boss, P., Roos, S., & Harris, D. L. (2011). Grief in the midst of uncertainty and ambiguity: An exploration of ambiguous loss and chronic sorrow. In R. A. Neimeyer, D. L. Harris, H. R. Winokuer, & G. F. Thornton (Eds.), *Grief and bereavement in contemporary society: Bridging research and practice* (pp. 163–175). Routledge/Taylor & Francis.

Roos, S. (2002). *Chronic sorrow: A living loss.* Brunner-Routledge.

103   *Now, the loss is clearer. I saw his "breath become air."*

Kalanithi, P. (2016). *When breath becomes air.* Random House.

Chapter 9: Loss and Change

105   *Change creates stress because it's an alteration in a steady state— doing something different or doing something in a different way.*

Boss, P. (1987). Family stress. In M. Sussman & S. Steinmetz (Eds.), *Handbook of marriage and the family* (pp. 695–723). Plenum Press.

Boss, P. (1988). *Family stress management: A contextual approach.* Sage.

Boss, P., Bryant, C., & Mancini, J. (2017). *Family stress management: A contextual approach* (3rd ed.). Sage. https://doi.org/10.4135/9781506352206

106 First-order change *means pushing harder on what you have been doing. It's more of the same, but putting more energy into it.* Second-order change *is what is now called thinking outside the box, taking a new direction.*

Watzlawick, P., Weakland, J. H., & Fisch, R. (1974). *Change: Principles of problem formation and problem resolution.* W. W. Norton.

106 *Second-order change is considered transformation for survival.*

Watzlawick, P., Weakland, J. H., & Fisch, R. (1974). *Change: Principles of problem formation and problem resolution.* W. W. Norton.

109 *The bubonic plague, 1346–1353, which killed about half of Europe's population, was followed by the Renaissance, with new ideas about art and science.*

Benedictow, O. J. (2018). *The Black Death, 1346–1353: The complete history.* Boydell Press.

Szalay, J. (2016, June 29). *The Renaissance: The "rebirth" of science and culture.* Live Science. https://www.livescience.com/55230-renaissance.html

109 *World War I, 1914–1918, and the flu epidemic of 1917–1918, which sickened one-third of the world's population with at least 50 million deaths worldwide and about 675,000 deaths in the United States alone.*

Centers for Disease Control and Prevention. (2019, March 20). *1918 pandemic (H1N1 virus).* https://www.cdc.gov/flu/pandemic-resources/1918-pandemic-h1n1.html

109 *What followed was the prosperous Roaring 20s, with advances in technology—telephones, radios, and the automobile.*

History.com Editors. (2020, August 12). *The Roaring 20s history.* https://www.history.com/topics/roaring-twenties/roaring-twenties-history

109   *The women's suffrage movement reignited and continued until 1920 when women won the right to vote.*

History.com Editors. (2020, August 15). *19th Amendment.* https://www.history.com/topics/womens-history/19th-amend-ment-1

109   *(Note that while in theory all women won the right to vote with the Nineteenth Amendment, in practice most Black women were prevented from voting until the Voting Rights Act was passed in 1965.)*

Jones, M. S. (2020). *Vanguard: How Black women broke barriers, won the vote, and insisted on equality for all.* Basic Books.

110   *World War II, 1939–1945, and the polio epidemic of the 1950s were followed by the turmoil and violence of the civil rights movement from 1954 to 1968 and beyond.*

History of Vaccines. (2021). *History of polio.* https://www.historyofvaccines.org/timeline/polio

History.com Editors. (2021, January 19). *Civil rights movement timeline.* https://www.history.com/topics/civil-rights-movement/civil-rights-movement-timeline

110   *Riots in Los Angeles followed, but the needed changes in the Los Angeles Police Department came slowly, nearly a decade later, and only after the federal government got involved.*

Lee, T., Schuppe, J., & Petulla, S. (2017, April 29). 25 years since Rodney King riots: Race, rebellion, and rebirth in South L.A. *NBC News.* https://www.nbcnews.com/news/us-news/ballad-south-l-race-rebellion-rebirth-n751471

110   *In 2018, Greta Thunberg represented an escalation of the climate change movement among the younger generations.*

Crouch, D. (2018, September 1). The Swedish 15-year-old who's cutting class to fight the climate crisis. *The Guardian.* https://www.theguardian.com/science/2018/sep/01/swedish-15-year-old-cutting-class-to-fight-the-climate-crisis

110   *2010–2019: The Defense of Marriage Act (DOMA) was declared*

unconstitutional in 2013, opening the path to federal recognition of same-sex marriage.

Barnes, R. (2013, June 26). Supreme court strikes down key part of Defense of Marriage Act. *Washington Post.* https://www.washingtonpost.com/politics/supreme-court/2013/06/26/f0039814-d9ab-11e2-a016-92547bf094cc_story.html

110 *2020: The year of the COVID-19 pandemic and George Floyd's murder; massive unrest and worldwide demonstrations in support of Black Lives Matter.*

Healy, J., & Searcey, D. (2020, May 31). Two crises convulse a nation: A pandemic and police violence. *New York Times.* https://www.nytimes.com/2020/05/31/us/george-floyd-protests-coronavirus.html

Khan-Cullors, P., & Bandele, A. (2017). *When they call you a terrorist: A Black Lives Matter memoir.* St. Martin's Griffin.

111 *2021: On January 6, 2021, the violent invasion of the U.S. Capitol by insurrectionists aiming to negate the outcome of the presidential election, execute the vice president and other lawmakers—and destroy essential democratic processes.*

Fandos, N., & Cochrane, E. (2021, January 6). After pro-Trump mob storms Capitol, congress confirms Biden's win. *New York Times.* https://www.nytimes.com/2021/01/06/us/politics/congress-gop-subvert-election.html

111 *Kamala Harris, the newly-elected vice president, broke several glass ceilings—first woman, first Black, and first Asian American to be elected vice president of the United States of America.*

Olorunnipa, T., & Linskey, A. (2021, January 20). Joe Biden is sworn in as the 46th president, pleads for unity in inaugural address to a divided nation. *Washington Post.* https://www.washingtonpost.com/politics/joe-biden-sworn-in/2021/01/20/13465c90-5a7c-11eb-a976-bad6431e03e2_story.html

111 *Juneteenth (June 19), commemorating the end of slavery for the entire United States, is made a national holiday.*

Karni, A., & Broadwater, L. (2021, June 17). Biden signs law making Juneteenth a federal holiday. *New York Times.* https://www. nytimes.com/2021/06/17/us/politics/juneteenth-holiday-biden.html

113   *But as James Baldwin wrote, in 1962, "Nothing can be changed until it is faced."*

Baldwin, J. (1962, January 14). As much truth as one can bear. *New York Times Book Review.*

113   *When they reached the I-35W bridge across the Mississippi River, a semitruck driver, not knowing the road was closed, almost ran into the marchers.*

Walsh, P., & Van Berkel, J. (2020. June 2). Truck driver wasn't aiming for protesters on 35W bridge, Minnesota authorities say. *Star Tribune.* https://www.startribune.com/truck-driver-didn-t-intend-to-hit-protesters-on-35w-bridge-state-officials-say/570925582/

Afterword

118   *Lawmakers and the vice president were threatened, five people died, many were hurt. Immense damage was done to the Capitol Building, costing over $30 million to repair.*

Chappell, B. (2021, February 24). *Architect of the Capitol outlines $30 million in damages from pro-Trump riot.* NPR. https://www.npr.org/sections/insurrection-at-the-capitol/2021 /02/24/970977612/architect-of-the-capitol-outlines-30-million-in-damages-from-pro-trump-riot

Healey, J. (2021, February 22). These are the 5 people who died in the Capitol riot. *New York Times.* https://www.nytimes .com/2021/01/11/us/who-died-in-capitol-building-attack.html

118   *As of now more than 570 defendants have been charged.*

Hymes, C., McDonald, C., & Watson, E. (2021, August 6). Seven months after the Capitol siege, more than 570 defendants have been arrested. *CBS News.* https://www.cbsnews.com/news/ us-capitol-riot-arrests-latest-2021-08-06/

118   *On April 20, 2021, an anxious crowd and worldwide press gathered in front of the Hennepin County Courthouse in Minneapolis to hear the jury's verdict. After about 10 hours of deliberation, it was announced, "Guilty, guilty, guilty." On all three counts of murder and*

manslaughter, the jurors unanimously found this white policeman guilty of unjustly killing a Black man.

Beaumont, P., & Jones, S. (2021, April 21). 'Guilty, guilty, guilty': World's media react to Chauvin trial verdict. *The Guardian.* https://www.theguardian.com/us-news/2021/apr/21/guilty-world-media-chauvin-trial-verdict-george-floyd-us-race-relations

Forgrave, R., & Rao, M. (2021, April 21). Conviction of Derek Chauvin: A moment of victory amid a history of injustice. *Star Tribune.* https://www.startribune.com/conviction-of-derek-chauvin-a-moment-of-victory-amid-a-history-of-injustice/600048330/

Forliti, A., Karnowski, S., & Webber, T. (2021, April 21). Jury's swift verdict for Chauvin in Floyd death: Guilty. *AP News.* https://apnews.com/article/derek-chauvin-convicted-george-floyd-killing-d93d1f9fc61a5261e179240dc16924dc

118 *On June 11, 2021, Darnella Frazier, whose video recording of George Floyd's murder went around the world, was awarded a Pulitzer Prize citation for citizen journalism.*

Hernandez, J. (2021, June 11). *Darnella Frazier, who filmed George Floyd's murder, wins an honorary Pulitzer.* NPR *News.* https://www.npr.org/2021/06/11/1005601724/darnella-frazier-teen-who-filmed-george-floyds-murder-wins-pulitzer-prize-citati

119 *As protestor Simone Hunter said, "It's not just about George Floyd. It's about all the unseen sh*t where we* don't *have the video."*

Mogelson, L. (2020, June 15). The heart of the uprising in Minneapolis. *The New Yorker.* https://www.newyorker.com/magazine/2020/06/22/the-heart-of-the-uprising-in-minneapolis

Index

About the Author

Pauline Boss, Ph.D., is renowned as the pioneer researcher and theorist of ambiguous loss, a term she coined in the 1970s. She has published over 100 peer-reviewed articles and chapters and 8 books, now translated into 17 languages. She was awarded Fellow in APA, AAMFT, and NCFR, and most recently received the AAMFT Emeritus Aweard for extraordinary work and leadership in marriage and family therapy. She has been a Visiting Professor at Harvard Medical School and University of Southern California, as well as Moses Professor at Hunter School of Social Work.

She has been interviewed by various media including CNN, Good Morning America, *The Atlantic*, *The New York Times*, *The Guardian*, *The Washington Post*, BBC, CBS, and NPR, among others, and over the past decades has been the go-to voice speaking to issues of national and international importance about ambiguous losses from 9/11 in New York to the missing airline in Malaysia in 2014, the 2011 tsunami in Fukushima, Japan, and most recently about the global pandemic in Europe, United Kingdom, Ireland, and Asia.